Sex.

Discovering Real Love in
a World of Counterfeits

BARBOUR
PUBLISHING

Sex.

Discovering Real Love in
a World of Counterfeits

Sexuality throws no light upon love, but only through love can we learn to understand sexuality.

EUGENE ROSENSTOCK-HUESSY

Only in a marriage—a marriage where love is—can sex develop into the delightfully positive force God meant it to be. Here is where the excitement of sex really is. When a man and a woman make a lifelong commitment to love and cherish each other, they are giving themselves the time they will need to dismantle the barriers of restraint, shyness, defensiveness, and selfishness that exist between all human beings. It cannot be done in a night or with a rush of passion. It takes time to know and be known.

COLLEEN TOWNSEND EVANS

INTRODUCTION

Love and Sex. . .the two words conjure up more distortions and misrepresentations than almost any other words in the English language. Some people confuse sex with love, and then others think there is no correlation between the two. No wonder few stop to consider that love and sex are created by God and are two of His most beautiful and gracious gifts.

Sex. was written to present the truth about love and sex from God's perspective and to help readers understand the many misconceptions that the world has about these important topics. As you read, it is our prayer that you will gain a new perspective, a right way of thinking, a holy point of view about a subject as old as the Garden of Eden. After all, love and sex were God's ideas to begin with!

THE WORLD SAYS:
"Love is a feeling."

GOD SAYS:
"Love is a decision."

"Love your neighbor as yourself."
MATTHEW 22:39

How realistic is God's Word? We're tempted to answer "not very" when confronted with Jesus' command to love everyone. After all, not everyone proves lovable. A few people even bring us grief or injury in return for our love. We may find it impossible to cultivate loving feelings toward certain individuals, so we dismiss Jesus' words as a noble, but unachievable, ideal.

Our mistake lies not in the content of Jesus' command to love, but in our definition of love. We commonly speak of love as an emotion: feelings of warmth and affection toward someone else. Romantic love implies even more—desire, delight, and joy in the presence of one special person. But life experience tells us that even the most intense feelings of love can change over time. If love isn't a decision, we'll have no convincing reason to continue a relationship after loving feelings have faded. If love is anything less than a decision, we'll feel justified in deciding others aren't lovable at all.

The kind of love Jesus spoke about transcends fleeting feelings. He modeled love in the mercy and compassion He showered on the largely thankless people who crowded around Him, hoping to see Him do something spectacular. He demonstrated love in His willingness to suffer crucifixion in payment of our sins, to die so we can escape eternal death, and rise from the grave so we can live a new life. Jesus personified love, a love outlasting any feeling or emotion.

Christlike love is a decision—a decision of the Holy Ghost at work in your life. When you forgive instead of condemn, listen rather than shout, show compassion without harboring anger, speak with respect, and treat with kindness, you love as Christ loves you. Decide to make Jesus' words real in your life today: Love with the kind of love that comes from the One who first loved you.

As the Father has loved me, so have I loved you; abide in my love.

JOHN 15:9 RSV

THE WORLD SAYS:
"Sex is just an act."

GOD SAYS:
"Sex joins two people—body, soul, and spirit."

Do you not know that he who unites himself with a prostitute is one with her in body? For it is said, "The two will become one flesh."

1 CORINTHIANS 6:16

An urban legend exposes our secret fears, fascinations, or desires in one short, compelling story. When it reaches enough people in the retelling, when it's printed in newspapers and pops up on the Internet, it assumes the status of fact.

In the same way, we hear messages about sex. TV and movies show unmarried couples enjoying sex as recreation. We read about celebrities who live with one person and then another, with a few affairs on the side. We date someone who expects sex to follow a good-night kiss. In the noise created by loudly repeated and readily accepted lies, it's easy to forget the truth.

God has spoken clearly about the nature of sex. While it's a physical act, it also has spiritual significance. Sex joins a man and a woman in one flesh, creating a physical, emotional, and spiritual bond between them. If you doubt the emotional and spiritual elements, take an objective look at the people you know who treat sex as a form of casual recreation. Do they exhibit joyful satisfaction with their lives? Do they appear at peace with themselves? Do you think they're having as much fun as they claim?

God wants you to take joyful satisfaction in the pleasure of sex. He wants you to experience His peace in your life, and He intends for you to take delight in sex. That's why He tells you what sex really means and how to experience it in a way that honors Him, your partner, and yourself. He made you a sexual person not so you can indulge in cheap thrills, but so you can know a supernatural and extraordinary unity with your partner in the bonds of holy matrimony.

If everyone says it, it may be true—or not. But if God says it, you can bet your life on it.

They become one flesh.

Genesis 2:24 RSV

THE WORLD SAYS:
*"Marriage is a
50/50 proposition."*

GOD SAYS:
*"Marriage is a
100/100 proposition."*

"With the measure you use, it will be measured to you."
LUKE 6:38

We like to feel we're getting a fair deal. We want to see others doing as much work as we do, giving to the community as actively as we give, and pulling their own weight—as we believe we are. It's only fair. But in taking these same expectations into marriage, we get something much less than a fair deal. We get disaster.

Think about what it takes to ensure a fair deal for both members of a married couple. Each needs to keep track of who did what and when. Did she clear the dishes from the dishwasher last week or did he? Did he put the clothes in the dryer yesterday or did she? And if he determines it's her turn—after all, it's only fair—he confronts her and tells her so. If she finds out she's vacuumed twice in a row—how unfair!—she accuses him of not taking his turn. Or maybe he'll be big and keep his opinion of her negligence to himself. Perhaps she'll not tell him he hasn't helped out in—count 'em!—three days. Resentment has just found fertile ground.

Christ doesn't give us what's fair. In our relationship with Him, He gives us everything. He doesn't ask us to meet Him 50/50. He doesn't count how many times we fail Him, disobey His commandments, or neglect our part of the bargain. Instead, He did everything we need to have a complete relationship with God. He died for our sins and earned for us His righteousness. He sends His Spirit to keep and nurture us in a holy, divine, grace-full relationship with Him. In return for what? Three percent of our time each week? Two percent of our income? One percent of our talent? No, God isn't getting a fair deal. . .but in His great love, He's not asking for one.

Today, talk to God about your willingness to give 100 percent plus. Anything less is less than what Christ has given you.

Christ loved us and gave himself up for us.

Ephesians 5:2 RSV

THE WORLD SAYS:
"Sex is just a casual form of recreation."

GOD SAYS:
"Sex is a pure expression of love within the bonds of marriage."

"Go and sin no more."
JOHN 8:11 NLT

On behalf of politicians or corporations, public relations spokespersons try to put their employers in the best possible light. They publicly articulate and clarify issues in which an officeholder or a company has a stake. When accusations of wrongdoing start flying, however, the PR job gets dicey. With reputations on the line or the possibility of indictments looming, savvy PR puts out alternative explanations and resorts to euphemisms to deflect attention from what really has happened.

We have full-blown, smart, and sophisticated PR departments working 24/7 to redefine sexual sin. First, media of all kinds offer glowing images of carefree, sexually active people enjoying each other, regardless of who's married—or not—to whom. Second, some friends, coworkers, and even family members see nothing wrong with sex outside of marriage. Finally, our own flesh urges us to give in—not to something called "sin," but to what "everybody's doing."

No PR statement fools God. He has defined good and evil, and His definitions don't change with the times or with the people involved and their specific circumstances. Without exception, He condemns adultery and fornication. And without exception, He offers forgiveness for sexual sins to the sinner who repents. To the repentant woman caught in the act of adultery, Jesus said, "Go and sin no more." Did she walk away suddenly free from all sexual desire? Scriptures report no such thing, and life experience tells us she most likely struggled with her passionate emotions and sexual desires. Nonetheless, Jesus' words still stood.

Will you find it easy to "go and sin no more"? No. God doesn't promise you it will be. But He does promise you His strength in times of temptation. He promises you His Holy Spirit to help you follow a sexually healthy lifestyle. He promises you His wisdom as you make decisions about how you express your God-given sexuality.

God has clearly defined sex. Listen and hear His voice.

I beg you not to surrender to those desires that fight against you.

1 PETER 2:11 CEV

THE WORLD SAYS:
"Just move in together. You don't need a piece of paper to prove your love."

GOD SAYS:
"There is no love without commitment."

"I know all the things you do, that you are neither hot nor cold. I wish you were one or the other! But since you are like lukewarm water, I will spit you out of my mouth!"

REVELATION 3:15–16 NLT

Extreme sports call for risks not everyone likes to take. From the comfort of our chairs, most of us are quite content to *ooh!* and *aah!* at the spectacle of someone else diving out of an airplane at thirteen thousand feet.

Christians often take a spectator position toward Christianity. We like being Christian, but sometimes we really don't want to participate. Unfortunately, risk-free Christianity is name-only Christianity. Genuine Christianity is a living, growing relationship with Christ. Like all relationships, it doesn't flourish without commitment. Jesus proved His commitment to us by walking among us to show us God in human flesh. He committed Himself to making us right with God by sacrificing Himself for our sins, winning our forgiveness, and earning our righteousness. That's commitment—extreme commitment! And He graciously sends His Spirit so we can live totally committed to Him.

In the same way, marriage is a living, growing relationship between a man and a woman. In marriage, you publicly declare your commitment to one other person. You voluntarily renounce all other options, putting away the distraction of other romantic interests to faithfully devote yourself to your spouse. In marriage, you and your spouse agree to close off for yourselves an easy out in times of trouble, stress, or disillusionment, giving your commitment a chance to grow roots and mature. In marriage, you and your spouse signal to the world you take the Christian message seriously—extremely seriously.

If it's genuine, your relationship with Christ requires your commitment to follow Him. Sometimes, in the eyes of the world, you'll be taking extreme risks for the sake of your faith. Your relationship with your partner works much the same way. In the eyes of the world, the two of you will make an extremely risky commitment to each other. It's called marriage.

Return to me.
MALACHI 3:7 CEV

THE WORLD SAYS:
*"Christianity is just
a bunch of rules."*

GOD SAYS:
*"My rules are not to burden
you—but to protect you."*

*Whoever is wise, let him heed these things and consider
the great love of the LORD.*
PSALM 107:43

Authoritarianism is considered passé. Dictatorial governments give way to more democratic forums. Top-down corporate structures flatten to delegate authority among department managers. Yesterday's lecturer now solicits students' views and opinions. Many parents allow children to make decisions at an early age. In all this, we need to keep in mind an important fact: God's authority still stands.

Our Creator knows best how to protect us from danger, hurt, and harm. He's aware of the changes in our society, but He also knows how little human nature has changed. God has not excused us from the authority of His fixed commandments in favor of society's shifting mores as the standard of our behavior. God has not opted to allocate some of His moral authority to us. Instead, God lights our way with His Word so we don't have to wander in the dark. Like an attentive and caring Father, God makes firm rules for us to follow. Sometimes we see the "why" of a rule, and sometimes we don't. Nonetheless, none are debatable.

Of course—children that we are—we rebel from time to time. We think we see a better, more convenient, way to do things. We consider a certain rule old-fashioned or not applicable to our situation. Or we see the point of a particular rule—for other people. Sooner or later, we find out to our sorrow that if we had heeded God's rule, we wouldn't be in the mess we're in. We find out from firsthand experience that God's authoritarianism works for our stability, peace, and protection.

Society will continue to change its mind about which rules are relevant and which are passé—that's the fickle nature of society. But God does not change His mind about His commandments, nor does He change His willingness to forgive every sinner who repents. That's the unchangeable nature of God.

*Throw yourselves wholeheartedly and full-time. . .
into God's way of doing things.*
ROMANS 6:13 MSG

SEX.

THE WORLD SAYS:
"If it feels good, do it."

GOD SAYS:
"Do good, even when it feels bad."

"See to it, then, that the light within you is not darkness. Therefore, if your whole body is full of light, and no part of it dark, it will be completely lighted, as when the light of a lamp shines on you."

LUKE 11:35–36

It has been said we can know our true character by what we do when no one's looking. Better yet, we can get a clear gauge of our character rating by what we think when things don't go our way. . .when work intrudes on play. . .when it's inconvenient to help out. . .when it would be easier, and much more pleasant, to go along with our own desires. How do you measure up?

God invites His people to develop a strong and mature character, and He gives us the means to do so. He gives us His Word so we can gain His wisdom in areas of thought, attitude, and behavior. He sends His Spirit to work in us the ability to apply His Word to the situations life brings our way. By His Spirit, we're enabled to make daily choices and decisions that build up God-pleasing character in us, even when tough choices present themselves.

No one enjoys putting aside personal desires in favor of higher principles. It's not thrilling to make a choice that requires our giving up of time or other resources. It's hardly a laugh a minute to follow a course of action that attracts the scorn and disparagement of our friends and coworkers. It feels even less rewarding when no one even knows we've made an unselfish decision, when we're doing something for someone else because we believe that's what God would have us to do! Yet it's the stuff of genuine, mature, godly character.

You're not alone in being tempted to do whatever comes naturally and seems the most pleasant thing to do. Everyone is tempted the same way. Not everyone, however, has the Spirit-given sight to see beyond self-indulgence. You do. Because of Christ, you aren't restricted to simply feeling good. In Him, you can do good, godly, and God-pleasing things. Even when no one—except God—is looking.

If you listen obediently to the Voice of God, your God, and heartily obey all his commandments that I command you today, God, your God, will place you on high, high above all the nations of the world.

DEUTERONOMY 28:1 MSG

THE WORLD SAYS:
"I love you because. . ."

GOD SAYS:
"I love you in spite of. . ."

He who does not love does not know God, for God is love.
1 JOHN 4:8 NKJV

Human love has reasons. Love's reasons range from ethereal: "because she makes me feel like a million dollars," to crass: "because he has a million dollars." God's love for people, however, has no reason. And because His love has no reason, it's often hard for us to get a handle on it. In fact, love without reason departs so radically from what we're used to, we frequently turn away from it altogether.

"How can God love me? Just look at the things I've done and the kind of person I am!" Yes, God knows. . .and He loves you anyway. Jesus, true God and true Man, was tempted just like you were, are, and will be until your last day. But for you, He led a perfect life. For you, He took on your sins and became your love-offering to God in payment for those sins. Jesus opened up God's love to you. Through Him, you have it. Why? Because of God's pure, no-reason love.

Yet some people insist on coming up with a "because" for God's love. They'll credit themselves with attributes deserving of God's love. Or they'll work themselves silly trying to earn God's love. Or they'll declare breezily, "God loves everybody," and walk away feeling pleased with such a meaningless sentiment. All these responses to God's divine love fail miserably. God's love has nothing to do with any attribute or contribution of people. It has everything to do with God himself. *God is love.*

Your humble acceptance of God's pure love for you brings you His freedom. In your freedom from the guilt of sin, the delusion of pride, the burden of scoring points with God, and the deception of platitudes, you're free to love others. You can love the way Christ loves you with no strings attached. In spite of personal foibles and failures. Because of love. Love. . . because God loves you.

My beloved friends, let us continue to love each other
since love comes from God.
1 JOHN 4:7 MSG

THE WORLD SAYS:
"How you look is everything."

GOD SAYS:
"You look on the outward appearance, but I look on the heart."

"The Lord does not look at the things man looks at. Man looks at the outward appearance, but the Lord looks at the heart."

1 Samuel 16:7

Appearance matters. While it's true that an intelligent mind may dwell inside an unkempt body, few people will stay around long enough to discover it. We demonstrate self-respect and respect for others when we groom ourselves as appropriate to the places we go, the people we meet, and the work we do.

But appearance isn't everything. When we start to equate appearance with worth, we're stepping into dangerous waters. We'll soon find ourselves dismissing anyone who doesn't look rich enough, educated enough, attractive enough, young enough, or interesting enough. We'll start seeing people through a filter of their perceived worth. . .quite unlike the way God sees.

In His ministry on earth, Jesus revealed how God sees us. As Jesus sat in the temple one day, He watched worshipers put their money into the treasury. Rich people contributed large sums, as expected. Then a poor widow came and dropped in two almost worthless coins. Yet Jesus commended the widow to His disciples, because she "has put in more than all the others. All these people gave their gifts out of their wealth; but she out of her poverty put in all she had to live on" (Luke 21:3–4).

God sees what's in the heart—love, compassion, sincerity, generosity. He's not fooled by a designer dress that conceals a selfish heart. Neither is He deceived by a thrift-store shirt that hides a mean and covetous spirit. Nor is He sidelined by a three-piece suit that masks a condescending attitude. He doesn't dictate that we wear a uniform, dress the same way, or look alike. He doesn't need to, because He's going to the heart of the matter.

God has given you your body for you to take care of as a good steward. Let your appearance express Christian moderation, godly modesty, and respect for yourself and others. Then let His Spirit clothe what really counts—your heart.

"Stop judging by mere appearances, and make a right judgment."
JOHN 7:24

THE WORLD SAYS:
"No one will know."

GOD SAYS:
"I see all things."

Does he not see my ways and count my every step?
JOB 31:4

A seemingly upstanding family man and church member is found to have committed a series of heinous crimes. A high school student described by her friends as "just a normal girl" keeps a blog in which she spins dark and violent fantasies. When the "other life" comes to light, neighbors gasp in disbelief. Family members grapple with shock, anger, and betrayal. He had another side to him. She lived a double life. How could this have happened?

God knows—and knows well—how it happened. It happened when one man thought he could scheme in secret, but soon began to enjoy his clever masquerade. It happened when she started dabbling in witchcraft, then grew emboldened to delve deeper into her private imaginings. It happens when we allow ourselves "just a peek" at a pornographic Web site. . . after all, who's to know? It happens when we sneak behind our partner's back to meet an attractive colleague. . .because no one will ever find out. It happens when we feed illicit desires and creep around in the shadows of sinful pleasures. Who sees? Maybe your family and friends don't. But God does.

The light of God's all-seeing eye brings both accusation and comfort. Accusation because His perfect holiness exposes private, hidden sins. Comfort because His fatherly compassion warms a heart grown cold in the shades of shame. Where we cower in secret, He graciously shines the light of His commandments so He can lead us out through repentance and forgiveness.

What comfort to know God sees all things! No matter in what murky corners your secret thoughts or actions may have led you, God sees you, and He desires to bring you into His light. Let His Spirit make you into one person—one authentic, truthful, and godly person. In Him, let the person your loved ones know be exactly the person you are.

Let the people turn from their wicked deeds. Let them banish from their minds the very thought of doing wrong! Let them turn to the LORD that he may have mercy on them. Yes, turn to our God, for he will abundantly pardon.

ISAIAH 55:7 NLT

THE WORLD SAYS:
*"Our marriage is over.
I don't love you anymore."*

GOD SAYS:
*"Love is a choice, and
marriage is for a lifetime."*

*"If serving the LORD seems undesirable to you, then choose for
yourselves this day whom you will serve. . . . As for me and my
household, we will serve the LORD."*

JOSHUA 24:15

Love them or loathe them, fairy tales flourish in our collective consciousness. We thrill to the news of a dashing prince winning the hand of a winsome young woman. We harbor the hope that someday great riches will come our way via the lottery or the bequest of a long-lost wealthy uncle. At the altar of holy matrimony, we like to think we'll live "happily every after."

If you still give credence to "happily ever after," it's safe to say you've been married less than a week. And if that's all you had—a vague and sentimental notion of love and happiness—your disillusionment probably will lead to the dissolution of your marriage. That's why God, who instituted marriage, never intended marriage to be based on fleeting feelings and fictitious ideals. He knows those kinds of marriages have nothing to hold them together after that first big quarrel and the stresses of family life. . .the intrusion of money problems, ill health, critical in-laws, and the office flirt. God instituted marriage based on the solid foundation of two people united as one in Him.

Your common purpose to serve Christ transcends the fluctuations of day-to-day moods and feelings. With the Lord as the center of your home, you both have Him to turn to in times of personal or family stress. You have direct access to the strength, compassion, and wisdom of One who cares about the two of you, who hears both sides of every argument, who never changes in His feelings for either of you. Neither of you need ever retreat to opposite corners in anger or disappointment, because you can always come together to your Lord and Savior in prayer.

A story too good to be true? It would be if told by anyone else but the One in whom rests your true and complete happiness. . .now and "ever after," too.

GOD told them, "I've never quit loving you and never will.
Expect love, love, and more love!"
JEREMIAH 31:3 MSG

THE WORLD SAYS:
"You have a right to be happy."

GOD SAYS:
"True happiness comes from surrendering your rights to Me."

Blessed is the man who fears the LORD,
who finds great delight in his commands.

PSALM 112:1

American inventor Thomas Edison said, "Opportunity is missed by most people because it is dressed in overalls and looks like work." Substitute "happiness" for "opportunity," and we have an equally valid observation.

We often miss true happiness because it comes dressed in the overalls of everyday life rather than the fancy garments of some future circumstance. While we imagine our happiness lies just beyond us. . .after graduation, after we land the perfect job, after we meet our one-and-only. . .happiness is very much a here-and-now occasion. In fact, if we're unable to recognize happiness today, we'll be no more able to recognize it tomorrow, no matter what tomorrow may bring. Sadly, it's possible to go through life without happiness because we've never learned what real happiness looks like.

In our eyes, happiness frequently looks like work. And, in a way, happiness is work. Not drudgery, but the sweet and satisfying labor of making a decision to be happy with who we are and what we have. Granted, a decision to be happy calls for effort, and it necessitates a change in perspective. When things aren't going well, it's easy to see only unhappiness. It's tempting to feel discontentment, restlessness, and dissatisfaction, which makes us even more unhappy. We blame circumstances. We fault our friends and coworkers. We accuse those closest to us without ever holding ourselves responsible for the work of our own happiness.

God promises contentment, peace, and satisfaction—true happiness—when we surrender ourselves to Him and His will. He knows what our happiness looks like. It's not nestled in some mirage of our own imaginations, but present in clear, observable, God-blessed reality.

What does happiness look like? It looks like who you are and what you have. It's happening where you live and with whom you share your life. True happiness looks like today—surrendered to the One who created happiness and gave you today.

[God says,] "I will satisfy. . .my people."
JEREMIAH 31:14

SEX.

THE WORLD SAYS:
"Go ahead;
God will forgive you."

GOD SAYS:
"Repent and sin no more."

Shall we sin because we are not under law but under grace? By no means! Don't you know that when you offer yourselves to someone to obey him as slaves, you are slaves to the one whom you obey— whether you are slaves to sin, which leads to death, or to obedience, which leads to righteousness?

ROMANS 6:15–16

The Christian life has been compared to a battle. Unlike battles fought between armies, neither truce nor compromise is possible. No win-win situation exists so both sides can save face. Even more, the Christian battle takes place every day in the life of those who sincerely want to follow Christ. It happens in your life when the desires of your flesh clash with the desires of your spirit.

When the flesh wins, you give in to your impulses. Sin gains authority over you, pacifying your spirit with the promise to repent later. And indeed, God will hear your words of repentance, and He will forgive you this time, next time, and the time after that for as long as you live. But when His Spirit has authority in your life, you don't want to keep sinning. His authority over you strengthens you for battle. The Holy Spirit clothes you with the winner's robes of godliness and self-control.

Left to yourself, you surely will lose the battle. The temptations of the flesh crush the best of human intentions, and human resolve falters and fails in the face of powerful desires. Only the Holy Spirit's work in you can equip you to win. He grants you the godly goal of wanting to live according to God's commandments, and He reminds you of God's will in times of temptation. If you fall, He lifts you up to repentance and enables you to believe in God's forgiveness through Jesus Christ.

If you're dating, a compromise with desire under the pretense of "going steady" or "we're both adults" means flesh has won. It doesn't have to be that way. Let the Holy Spirit bring you to the cross of Jesus Christ in repentance. Let Him lead you to the empty tomb for a celebration of His victory over sin and death. Win the battle—you can, because He has won the war.

God knows how to rescue the godly from evil trials.
2 PETER 2:9 MSG

THE WORLD SAYS:
"I'll change him/her after we get married."

GOD SAYS:
"Work on yourself."

Why worry about a speck in your friend's eye when you have a log in your own? How can you think of saying, "Let me help you get rid of that speck in your eye," when you can't see past the log in your own eye? . . . First get rid of the log from your own eye; then perhaps you will see well enough to deal with the speck in your friend's eye.

MATTHEW 7:3–5 NLT

Most of us find ourselves at one time or another meddling in someone else's business. We confidently tell our best friend what she's doing wrong in her relationships. We boldly outline what steps we would take if we were walking in our boss's shoes. We dutifully assign ourselves the job of fixing real or perceived shortcomings of people closest to us, most particularly those of our partner.

Let's take an objective look at ourselves as meddlers. We've positioned ourselves as an authority on the most intimate matters of someone else's life. No surprise, our presumption brings no thanks but breeds resentment on the part of the other person. And because of his or her justified resentment, our meddling meets with rejection. Any attempt to change the behavior of others with advice and nagging, critical remarks, and "helpful" reminders proves futile.

Fruitful change takes place when we start with ourselves. In the light of God's Word, we learn to humbly admit our weaknesses and willingly accept our need for improvement. In doing so, we not only gain self-knowledge, but we find it easier to empathize with others and the inner struggles they face. We realize how difficult it can be to reverse habits and perceptions etched into the memories, emotions, actions, and reactions of a lifetime. With the help of the Holy Spirit, however, real change can and does take place. By the Spirit's power alone, we change into fit and productive servants of God in His kingdom on earth.

When you show yourself willing and able to change, you influence others. Your visible growth may inspire someone who has given up hope, or who despairs of ever overcoming personality flaws or self-destructive habits. You put yourself in a credible position to offer advice when asked or help where needed. After all, you've been there. You know what it takes.

The God who started this great work in you [will] keep at it and bring it to a flourishing finish.
PHILIPPIANS 1:6 MSG

THE WORLD SAYS:
"Monogamy is old-fashioned."

GOD SAYS:

"One woman for one man and one man for one woman is My model for the home and society as a whole."

Drink water from your own well—share your love only with your wife. Why spill the water of your springs in public, having sex with just anyone? You should reserve it for yourselves. Don't share it with strangers.

PROVERBS 5:15–17 NLT

God established marriage as a lifelong union between one man and one woman to benefit husband and wife. In marriage, both members of the couple learn to trust each other in a stable, committed relationship. Each receives the exclusive love of the other expressed in mutually satisfying sexual intimacy. Marriage contributes to the physical and emotional health of husband and wife. As such, marriage provides the best environment for the raising of children.

In our sin-filled world, however, God's intention for marriage has become neglected, ignored, and distorted. Men and women enter marriage without a serious commitment to remain faithful to each other. Couples opt to dissolve their marriage rather than seek and pledge themselves to reconciliation. Yet God offers forgiveness to those who repent of sins committed within and against marriage, and He offers strength to those who have been victimized by these sins. If you find yourself in either situation, turn to Him for your help. In Him alone is your peace, healing, and restoration.

God not only tells us about marriage but models marriage in His relationship with us. He has committed Himself to us for life, eternal life. In Jesus Christ, He has intimately connected Himself with us. He desires to hear the sound of our voices, and He invites our thoughts, needs, fears, and confidences. Faith in Him boosts our sense of well-being because we know who we are (His), why we're here (to serve Him), and where we're going (heaven). Our God-established relationship with Him in Jesus is the best environment for a full and satisfying life here on earth.

Examine your attitude toward marriage. Does it reflect God's attitude toward you? Are you as committed to the marriage relationship as God is committed to you? Let His Word—not the world—inform you and guide you concerning the God-given gift of marriage.

The one who calls you is faithful.
1 THESSALONIANS 5:24

THE WORLD SAYS:
"Practice safe sex."

GOD SAYS:
"The only safe sex—outside of marriage—is no sex at all."

*"From within, out of men's hearts, come. . .sexual immorality. . .
[and] adultery.. . . These evils come from inside and
make a man 'unclean.' "*

MARK 7:21, 23

To get money, a man and a woman decide to rob a bank. They spend time figuring out the best way to pull off their heist without getting caught. Having decided, they commit the crime and successfully evade the police. Whew! Well, not really. Every knock at the door causes him to jump. . .every passing car sends her a shiver of fear. They wonder why having all the money they've ever wanted isn't as much fun as they thought it would be.

To satisfy their sexual desires, an unmarried man and woman decide to practice safe sex. They investigate the contraceptive devices and health protections available to them and decide what they'll use. Having made their selection, they become sexually active and do, indeed, avoid pregnancy and STDs. But a skipped period panics her. An unfamiliar rash alarms him. Both feel emotionally uneasy. They wonder why having sex whenever they want to isn't as much fun as they thought it would be.

Those who teach safe sex are as helpful as those who would promote risk-free bank robbery. Safe sex leaves out the glaring fact that we're spending time and effort figuring out how to do something we shouldn't be doing in the first place. No matter how overwhelming our debts, robbing a bank isn't a wise way to pay off creditors. No matter how powerful our desire, sex outside of marriage isn't a wise, healthful, or godly way to handle feelings. Sex, like money, works for our good when it's used and enjoyed as God intended. Used any other way, we're taking what doesn't rightfully belong to us. We'll find ourselves sated instead of satisfied, anxious instead of content, fretfully guilty instead of freely rejoicing.

The Holy Spirit counsels self-control. He knows you're more—much more—than a collection of runaway hormones. He's not afraid of the word *abstinence*. Are you?

Sin can't tell you how to live. After all, you're not living under that old tyranny any longer. You're living in the freedom of God.
ROMANS 6:14 MSG

THE WORLD SAYS:
"If you really love me, you'll prove it."

GOD SAYS:
"Love doesn't force itself on others."

"God so loved the world that he gave his one and only Son, that whoever believes in him shall not perish but have eternal life."

JOHN 3:16

The greatest Lover of all time never forced Himself on the object of His love. He wooed His Old Testament people Israel with tender words of invitation, promise, forgiveness, and assurance. He protected them, strengthened them, and showered them with His blessings. No matter how many times they fell away from Him and took other lovers, their Lover waited for them to return.

Jesus Christ never forced Himself on anyone. Instead, Jesus invited men and women to follow Him. He taught His disciples through words and example, revealed to them His divine powers, and endured suffering and death on the cross because of His love for the world. Nonetheless, many of His beloved people walked away. And many still do. We have the power to reject the One who loves us beyond any human conception of love.

Though our heavenly Father has a right to our love— didn't He create us? Doesn't He preserve us? Doesn't He continue to bless us?—yet He never forces Himself on us. Instead, He provides His Word, in which He reveals His great love. He fills the hearts of His servants to spread the Good News through word and action. He sends His Spirit to work in us faith in Jesus' sacrificial love for us. We know and experience true love from the One who *is* love.

Love distorted by sin restricts freedom. It binds its victim with demands and ultimatums. It spawns fear, hurt, hate, distrust, and self-destruction. Godly love, on the other hand, respects the selfhood of the beloved. It thrives in freedom to give and receive. It never seeks the person's harm, but only the good of the beloved.

How would you measure your ability to give and receive love? In Christ, you have the freedom to love willingly. . . because He freely and willingly loves you.

Mostly what God does is love you. Keep company with him and learn a life of love. Observe how Christ loved us. His love was not cautious but extravagant. He didn't love in order to get something from us but to give everything of himself to us. Love like that.

Ephesians 5:2 MSG

THE WORLD SAYS:
"You should be free to express your sexuality."

GOD SAYS:
"Only through love can you understand your sexuality."

How beautiful you are and how pleasing,
O love, with your delights!
Song of Songs 7:6

If you want to read a book brimming with romance, intimacy, passion, and yes, sex, read the Old Testament book Song of Songs. A wedding poem, Songs celebrates the intense physical passion and deep spiritual bond between a bride and groom. It also paints a picture of God's committed and passionate love for us, His people.

Leaving little to the imagination, the inspired writer debunks the erroneous idea that sex is something to hide, something to be ashamed of. The explicit verses belie the popular notion of Christians as prudes, fearful of their own desires, repressed by the rigors of abstinence prior to marriage, and frustrated by the demands of monogamy. Not so! Abstinence in single life frees us from the emotional turmoil and physical risks of promiscuity. Purity in married life frees us to delight in and enjoy lovemaking in a fulfilling, committed relationship.

God's love for you is like the passionate love of a groom for his bride. He's fully committed to you. In the mystery of Jesus' perfect life, His willing death on the cross, and His victorious resurrection from the dead, God demonstrates the extent of His commitment to you. In the work of His Holy Spirit in your heart, God confirms His intimate, personal, spiritual love for you. Your secure trust in God's love for you opens you to love and be loved.

Just as you cannot appreciate God's love for you without faith in Him, neither can you experience the joy of lovemaking outside the bonds of marriage. Outside marriage, sex loses its sacred significance and holy meaning. Shame and hurt distort sex, lessening its value and cheapening its purpose. How distant from the exuberant, confident, joyous love of the bride and groom in the book of Songs!

God gave your sexuality to you as a gift. Let your God-pleasing response be your gift to Him.

Then I'll marry you for good—forever! I'll marry you true and proper, in love and tenderness.

Hosea 2:19 msg

THE WORLD SAYS:
"Your spouse must respect your rights."

GOD SAYS:
"Submit to one another in love."

[Submit] to one another in the fear of God.
Ephesians 5:21 nkjv

If you want to draw the world's scorn, mention the word *submission*. Suddenly the conversation leaps to portray a wimp of a wife forced to bow to her husband's whims—to a brute of a husband brandishing his right to beat and berate his family at will. From there, the whole biblical conception of marriage crumbles in the "light" of women's liberation and equal rights.

In one widely misunderstood and misquoted section of his letter to the church in Ephesus, Paul has borne the brunt of condemnation, contempt, and outright dismissal. As with any portion of scripture, serious readers seek its God-given meaning within its Spirit-inspired context. Paul wrote to the Ephesians a letter of encouragement and advice. He urged unity within the congregation and the employment of diverse gifts and talents for the good of all. Paul then invited believers to look to Christ as their example in their relationships. He directed their attention to their most intimate relationship, that is, the family relationship. Here he counseled submission.

Why submission? Not so wives can duck out of responsibility for their decisions, health, and well-being. Not so husbands can browbeat wives. But submission of both to Christ, purely out of reverence for Christ and because of what He has done for husbands, wives, sons, daughters. . .all of us. He submitted to His Father's will purely out of love for us and so we could have a loving relationship with Him. How can we do any less?

How indeed? By ourselves, we're unable to submit to God, much less to one another. Our desire for status, entitlements, rights, and equality as the world defines these things echoes in our ears. His Spirit alone has the power to turn our eyes to God and to one another in a spirit of sacred submission. From Him, we know what submission means because He uses the word in His Word.

Submit to the Father of our spirits and live!
HEBREWS 12:9

THE WORLD SAYS:
*"Once you're married,
the relationship takes care
of itself."*

GOD SAYS:
*"Love is strong,
but it's vulnerable to neglect."*

Give, and it will be given to you.
LUKE 6:38 NKJV

Double-stitched seams. Tight weave. Easy care. Wash and wear. If you're the parent of young children, you probably look for these qualities in the clothes you buy for them and maybe even in the clothes you buy for yourself. But applied to marriage, these same qualities tell only half the story.

Wedding vows along with a legally binding contract act like a double-stitched seam. The stresses of daily living, however, constantly tug at it. Responsibilities pull one way; arguments, anger, and resentment pull another. Children, finances, and work-related challenges yank seams in all directions. If left untended, stitches tear and rip, leaving gaps and weakened seams.

In the tight weave of love's first passions and sexual intimacy, the fabric of marriage seems extraordinarily durable. Yet attraction for someone else, pornography, and sexual perversions conspire to soil and weaken even the finest, strongest fibers. Left to work abusive wear, sin unravels marriages in faithlessness, distrust, and betrayal.

The security of commitment means relaxation—no more dating, no more searching, no more vying for the eye of that special person. Easy care! But not "no care." Taking a spouse's love for granted, dismissing his or her needs in favor of work, hobbies, rest, or recreation, disregarding his or her qualities and contributions put wrinkles in marriage. Unless ironed out immediately, distorting wrinkles settle in for good.

Once soiled, even the most easy-care fabric requires laundering. The ability of husbands and wives to say "I'm sorry" washes the marriage relationship in the cleansing waters of forgiveness. Couples acknowledge their sins before God and acknowledge them before each other, both granting and accepting forgiveness. With frequent washing, they wear their marriage in a spirit of peace and gratitude.

A God-centered marriage has double-stitched seams and a tight weave. It's easy care, wash, and wear. Tended with love, the garment will last a lifetime.

Guard the treasure you were given! Guard it with your life.
1 TIMOTHY 6:20 MSG

THE WORLD SAYS:
"Dress to attract."

GOD SAYS:
"Dress tastefully and modestly."

We also know that law is made not for the righteous but for. . .rebels.
1 TIMOTHY 1:9

God's not asking us to wear head-to-toe robes, loose dresses, or dark suits. We're free to wear what we want, right? After all, God looks at the heart.

True. But men and women look at each other. Through our choice of clothing, we imply certain messages. When our clothing follows too closely the questionable fads and trends of the world, we're in danger of coming across as worldly, proud, or sexually available. "But I don't mean it," protests the mini-skirted young woman. "I just want to be fashionable. All my friends are wearing skirts this short!" "Hey," says the guy with studs in his eyebrows and a ring in his nose, "it doesn't mean a thing. It's just a harmless fad." From their point of view, they're telling the truth. From the point of view of others, however, another conclusion might come to mind.

Extreme or overdone styles of clothing, jewelry, and grooming describe the wearer as someone who spends a great deal of time and money on appearance. Correctly or incorrectly, we infer the person has less interest in others and gives less time to serious subjects than the more modestly and appropriately attired individual. A woman who goes out in a skintight dress shouldn't be shocked to find herself the object of unwanted attention. A man who struts through the office wearing an unbuttoned shirt and heavy gold jewelry shouldn't wonder why he's not offered the next promotion. Immodest attire says loudly and clearly: "Look at me, but don't take me seriously! I'm just here for the shopping."

God wants your attire to tell a different story. You're *in* the world but not *of* the world. You don't have to bow to every worldly trend. You're aware of the signals you send with your appearance, so reflect who you really are: God's beloved child. It's your sacred privilege to dress accordingly.

Your inner self, the unfading beauty of a gentle and quiet spirit. . .is of great worth in God's sight.

1 PETER 3:4

THE WORLD SAYS:
"You must be in a relationship to be happy."

GOD SAYS:
"True joy comes from knowing Me."

"The joy of the Lord is your strength."
Nehemiah 8:10

Life begins at. . .when? Twenty? Forty? Sixty? Many of us go through the years of our lives believing "things will get better" when we reach a certain age. Or enter a particular salary range. Or meet that special someone. Then, surely, we can start living!

If the flaw in this kind of thinking isn't evident to you, just ask an older person and hear the plain truth: Time goes by too quickly for you to waste a moment waiting to "start living." And unfortunately, when your desired situation arises, you will find it doesn't hold all the happiness potential you had anticipated. So you put off happiness again, waiting for another change. The habit of putting life on hold can itself last a lifetime. As the Greek proverb notes, "They who laugh not in the morning, laugh not at noon."

A healthy attitude toward life seeks happiness in all situations. A godly outlook never withholds gratitude until "everything's perfect," because God's wisdom tells us everything will never be perfect this side of heaven. If you're single right now, explore all the ways available to you to freely serve others. Find true happiness in being who you are, as you are. Ironically, your engagement with life will work to draw people to you. Happy people attract people—so it's a fair guess you won't be single for long! In addition, you'll realize an important truth about the nature of happiness: It comes from within.

God wants His people to be a happy people. Therefore, He doesn't restrict happiness to one group of people but makes it available to the young as well as to the old, to the poor as well as to the rich, to the single man or woman as well as to the married couple. Ask Him now to help you discover the true and lasting happiness of being you.

He satisfies the thirsty and fills the hungry with good things.
PSALM 107:9

THE WORLD SAYS:
*"Two consenting adults
should be free
to do anything."*

GOD SAYS:
"Honor Me with your body."

*Do you not know that your body is a temple of the Holy Spirit, who
is in you, whom you have received from God? You are not your own;
you were bought at a price. Therefore honor God with your body.*

1 CORINTHIANS 6:19–20

Much as Hollywood might like to think otherwise, sex is God's idea. He created male and female, giving each a specific sexual identity, or foundation. On this foundation, you grew up as a boy or a girl and matured into a man or a woman.

The Holy Spirit builds on the foundation of your God-given sexuality. As a man or a woman of God, you serve Him in the things you do. . .most likely in specific ways God had in mind for you alone. In His Spirit, you enjoy certain material gifts and spiritual blessings God has showered on you, gifts and blessings delightful to you as a man, as a woman. You express your gratitude to Him through your physical presence, your prayers, and your songs of praise.

How you maintain your body, then, becomes not simply a physical matter, but also a spiritual one. God made your body, and He sent His Son to redeem it from everlasting death. His Spirit dwells in you, enabling you to act out your faith in myriad ways and by countless means. So what you eat matters, and how much you drink matters. Whether or not you exercise matters, and your choice to use or abstain from illegal drugs matters. And what you do in bed matters.

All this matters because your body is not your own, but His. The Holy Spirit lives in you. In fact, He calls your body His temple. He calls the body of your Christian spouse His temple, also. What you do together—how you express your sexuality within the bonds of marriage—can either enhance the temple of the Holy Spirit, or degrade it. . .build it up or tear it down. On the foundation of your sexuality, you're free to do most anything. . .but there may be some things you simply choose not to do.

I plead with you to give your bodies to God. Let them be a living and holy sacrifice—the kind he will accept. When you think of what he has done for you, is this too much to ask?

Romans 12:1 nlt

THE WORLD SAYS:
"Flirting is a fun pastime."

GOD SAYS:
"Flirting is a form of deceit."

*Obscene stories, foolish talk, and coarse jokes—these are not for
you. Instead, let there be thankfulness to God.*
EPHESIANS 5:4 NLT

"Loose lips might sink ships." The World War II poster reminded soldiers to be watchful—watchful about what they disclosed when they wrote letters home and watchful about what they said as they talked to their family and friends while on leave. Chance remarks, candid answers, or careless boasts could reveal military strategy to the enemy, resulting in harm or death to US troops.

Loose lips—flirtatious kidding, risqué double entendres, suggestive poses—serve the war-hardened, sworn enemies of godliness. Though we may consider ourselves innocently dabbling in "adult" conversation among friends, we're actually skipping right over to enemy ranks. Dirty talk stems not from a mind fixed on Christ, but from a mind entertained by lustful thoughts. Obscene jokes and seductive come-ons reflect a heart mired in the world's values, a spirit unwilling to give up the temporary thrill of worldly conduct for the dignity of godly behavior.

Careless talk and flirtatious manners can damage, even shipwreck, lives. Smutty jokes embarrass and offend many people. . .even those who feel obliged to laugh. Teasing can unleash indescribable anguish on its victim. A playful overture may be taken quite seriously by its recipient, resulting in hurt feelings, anger, and disappointment. The constant need to deliver a witty double entendre (and give one back in kind) degrades conversation to a game of one-upmanship. Every "win" gained with such irresponsible behavior brings a multitude of losses—loss of reputation, loss of self-restraint, loss of judgment, loss of Christian friends, loss of Christian identification.

We're called to be imitators of Christ. Is it easy as our co-workers guffaw at a coarse joke? Is it effortless when we'd like others to notice our sophistication, our wit, our sex appeal? No. The document on the requirements of self-censorship given to soldiers stated bluntly: "This takes guts." Yes, this takes guts. . .and a Spirit-empowered, Christ-centered choice to remain faithful to your God.

Love doesn't strut.

1 CORINTHIANS 13:4 MSG

THE WORLD SAYS:
"If you don't approve of homosexuality, you are filled with hate."

GOD SAYS:
"I hate the sin of homosexuality, but I love the homosexual."

If we confess our sins to him, he is faithful and just to forgive us and to cleanse us from every wrong.

1 JOHN 1:9 NLT

When we're doing something we shouldn't be doing, we don't want anyone reminding us of the fact. When the truth hurts, we naturally want to avoid the truth.

God's clear and plain word about homosexuality conflicts with what we'd like to think. Most of us study, work, and socialize with homosexuals. Some of us have a family member who has identified himself or herself as homosexual. Perhaps we have doubts about our own sexual preference, or we would like to choose a partner of our own sex. Because we don't want to offend anyone, appear judgmental or intolerant, or deride someone else for a tendency we may suspect within ourselves, we avoid the truth. We say nothing at all.

Yet speak we must, for God has spoken. Though homosexual couples are becoming increasingly accepted in our society, and even within Christian congregations, God calls homosexual behavior a sin. What God has created for one man and one woman united in marriage becomes warped in the sexual acts of same-sex couples. Those who persist in this sin after having heard God's Word (as in the case of any other sin) risk God's judgment.

Telling an unpopular truth isn't easy. To begin, pray. Pray for the person, asking for the Holy Spirit to give you an opportunity and the wisdom to bring God's Word to his or her attention. Resist the temptation to express disgust or evoke hellfire. In a caring tone of voice, share your convictions founded in God's Word. Clearly affirm the person with the gospel message of forgiveness through Jesus Christ and remind him or her of new life promised through the power of the Holy Spirit. Listen with understanding and compassion. Encourage the individual's desire to move away from the homosexual lifestyle, and assist in any way you can.

Sometimes, the truth hurts. . .but in the Truth rests freedom.

You are near, O LORD, and all your commands are true.

PSALM 119:151

THE WORLD SAYS:
"Some people are born homosexual."

GOD SAYS:
"In the beginning, I made them male and female."

God created people in his own image; God patterned them after himself; male and female he created them.

GENESIS 1:27 NLT

Here's a controversial issue. Some experts say homosexuals are born, not made. Therefore he or she should be free to live a gay lifestyle. Other experts disagree, saying homosexuals decide on homosexuality and choose to live a gay lifestyle.

God's Word doesn't tell us who's right. Scriptures do tell us, however, that He has set boundaries on sexual expression. God, who created sex, restricts sex to one man and one woman within holy matrimony. He tells us to avoid lustful thoughts, whether these thoughts focus on a person of the same sex or the opposite sex. He warns us not to seek out and cultivate a sexual relationship motivated by lust and self-gratification; with someone already married; with a close relative; with a man if you're a man or with a woman if you're a woman. Each of us must answer to God for our sexual stewardship.

God signed no waivers for those who, for whatever reason, identify themselves as gay. Has God, then, doomed homosexuals to a life of loneliness? No. For gays and others who cannot or choose not to marry, God provides the gift of celibacy. In our sex-obsessed society, celibacy may seem a sorry gift, but from God's hands, it can be a witness, a blessing, and a life of satisfaction and fulfillment. A person committed to celibacy for the sake of Christ sends a true countercultural signal to young people pressured to become sexually active. A celibate's godly example demonstrates the possibility of wholeness outside of being a couple. Without obligation to one person, a celibate freely serves others in his or her family, church, and community. Often, God blesses a celibate person with the gift of a meaningful, long-lasting celibate friendship of the same or opposite sex.

Born or made? Ultimately, it doesn't matter. You were born God's child, and He has made you His own.

If [a person] has decided firmly not to marry and there is no urgency and he can control his passion, he does well not to marry.
1 CORINTHIANS 7:37 NLT

THE WORLD SAYS:
"If your marriage isn't fulfilling, you should get out."

GOD SAYS:
"If your marriage isn't fulfilling, start treating your spouse like you did when it was fulfilling."

I opened for my lover, but my lover had left; he was gone. My heart sank at his departure. I looked for him but did not find him. I called him but he did not answer.

Song of Songs 5:6

It's inevitable—after the honeymoon, things change. No longer can you and your beloved spend days and nights in a romantic haven, free of responsibilities. As you settle into your daily routine back home, work cuts deeply into the time you have alone with your spouse. When children join your household, their needs often trump Mom and Dad's romantic interests. Time itself takes the edge off newlyweds' passionate desire.

Before we bemoan the demands of modern society and the stress of family life, let's check God's Word. Song of Songs, written about 970 B.C., eulogizes passionate love between a bride and groom. But there comes a point in the poem where they struggle with the absence of passion, followed by emotional and physical desertion. If left unnoticed and untended, the situation could deteriorate into a lifeless marriage—or no marriage at all. The newlyweds in Songs take quick action to reclaim their love.

If you find yourself feeling less than fulfilled in your relationship—or if you think your spouse feels unfulfilled—it's time to reclaim your love. Sit down together for an open, honest discussion. What's missing now that you shared in the past? What can you do to recapture some of the romance and magic of earlier years? Do you make time to give thoughtful attention to each other's needs? How much effort do you give to making your marriage work as opposed to the effort expended on outside interests?

After the honeymoon's over, things will change. Together, pray for the Lord's blessing on your marriage. Put Christ at the center of your household, then look to Him for guidance as your love for each other deepens, grows, and matures. Be willing to ask for and receive forgiveness from Christ and from each other. Make daily devotions and weekly worship the center of your day and week. Let things change. . .for the better.

> *I found the one my heart loves.*
> *I held him and would not let him go.*
> SONG OF SONGS 3:4

THE WORLD SAYS:
"It is too risky to get married without knowing that you are sexually compatible."

GOD SAYS:
"It is too risky to marry a sexually promiscuous person."

[Love] always protects.
1 CORINTHIANS 13:7

At first glance, cohabitation seems like a good idea. "Try it before you buy it." But closer examination reveals that what's wise advice concerning your decision to purchase a car proves patently unwise concerning your decision to move in with your sweetheart before the wedding day.

Studies conducted over the past twenty-five years conclude that cohabitation before marriage does not prevent divorce after marriage. In fact, some studies find cohabiting couples put themselves at far greater risk of divorce than couples who never lived together before marriage. The studies suggest several reasons. Those who consent to cohabit don't value the commitment of marriage to a high degree. For Christians, committing the sin of sex outside marriage makes the sin of divorce that much easier. And the choice of cohabitation over marriage reveals a preference for individuality over union, of personal freedom over unconditional love.

Cohabiting couples who finally marry find marriage doesn't magically fix problems in their relationship. In fact, cohabitation works to erode the marriage bond. A lingering attachment to a past live-in partner or guilt over a previous relationship enters the marriage. Jealousy of past partners taints current love and plants reasonable doubt about the faithfulness of one spouse for the other. Furthermore, some single men and women avoid a romantic relationship with someone who's been sexually promiscuous. They know strong feelings rarely "let bygones be bygones."

If you're tempted to confuse your beloved with an automobile, prayerfully consider what God says about true love. Love is not taken on a trial basis, but given unconditionally. It doesn't try out several to determine its satisfaction, but commits to one and finds its satisfaction. It doesn't opt out, citing the "lemon law," but remains in every situation. Love—true love—is neither bought nor sold, neither used nor a user. . . but a lover.

Don't lose your grip on Love and Loyalty. Tie them around your neck; carve their initials on your heart.

PROVERBS 3:3 MSG

THE WORLD SAYS:
"Finding a mate is a game you must learn to play."

GOD SAYS:
"I brought Eve to Adam. I can bring your spouse to you if you will ask Me."

"Ask and it will be given to you; seek and you will find; knock and the door will be opened to you. For everyone who asks receives; he who seeks finds; and to him who knocks, the door will be opened."

MATTHEW 7:7–8

How to land a stud of a man. . .how to snag a sexy woman. Go to your local magazine counter, newspaper rack, or Internet site for a plethora of tips and advice on the subject. Get a few of your single friends together if you want a personalized touch. From a myriad of sources, you can gather information ranging from helpful to manipulative to ridiculous. Are you willing to let these voices determine how you go about finding your future husband or wife?

Many singles do. Christian singles beyond a certain age despair of ever meeting Mr. or Ms. Right, so they lower their standards. Maybe they downplay the role faith plays in their life. Perhaps they adopt some of the tricks they see their co-workers use to advantage. Or they decide no suitable person will ever show up at the singles' group at church, so they start frequenting bars to expand their territory. Consider the consequences! Granted, you may very well meet someone attractive to you. But who are you attracting? And are you presenting your true self to the other person?

When you believe you're ready to meet the person with whom you will share your life, take the matter up with God, the Creator and Giver of life. He invites you, His child, to come to Him as to a loving father. Humbly and confidently, lay your heart's desire at His feet. Come daily with your earnest supplication, and daily put the matter in His hands. Then go about your day with eyes open, seeking out and accepting His will in your life.

Be the kind of person whose words and actions attract godly people. Be ready to welcome the answer God has for you. Keep on praying! Your heavenly Father has promised to hear you. He gives you in His own time what He knows will work out best for you.

Trust GOD from the bottom of your heart; don't try to figure out everything on your own. Listen for GOD's voice in everything you do, everywhere you go; he's the one who will keep you on track.

PROVERBS 3:5–6 MSG

THE WORLD SAYS:
"Laughing at your sweetheart's quirks is innocent fun."

GOD SAYS:
"Love encourages. It does not discourage."

Love is kind.

1 CORINTHIANS 13:4

"Can't you take a joke?" If you find yourself hearing or saying those words, it's time to talk about teasing. While good-natured banter often marks a loving relationship, teasing signals a troubled relationship. If your date or spouse routinely humiliates you in the guise of "joking," you have an unhealthy relationship. If your humor revolves around your sweetheart's personality, foibles, or shortcomings, step back and consider the quality of your love.

God loves you, and His words to you are loving words. He never laughs at you for your weaknesses or limitations, but He sends His Spirit to help you overcome them. Instead of humiliating you in front of others by publicizing your sins, His Spirit enters the privacy of your heart to show you His way, invites you to repentance, and restores you to fellowship with Him. In scripture, He speaks to you with words of comfort, encouragement, and kindness. He speaks of you with love.

The quality of God's love sets the standard for the quality of love you give to others and the love you receive from others. If you feel yourself unworthy of such love—if you accept hurtful teasing and unkind jokes from others—turn to your heavenly Father and learn from Him your true worth, your incomparable value. You're His precious child for whom His only Son lived among us, suffered, died, and rose from the grave. In Christ, you have dignity, and you deserve respect.

If you hurl hurtful words in the name of humor, examine your true motivation. Is a laugh from the crowd worth your loved one's hurt? Is your loved one's reputation a fair price for the chance to get in a witty remark? If your answer makes you uncomfortable, good. God is at work in you, ready to forgive you and help you in the ways of love. . .true love. And that's no joke.

People who. . .[say,] "I didn't mean it, I was only joking," are worse than careless campers who walk away from smoldering campfires.
PROVERBS 26:18–19 MSG

THE WORLD SAYS:
"Faith doesn't make any difference in a marriage."

GOD SAYS:
"Faith makes all the difference in marriage."

They were from nations about which the LORD had told the Israelites, "You must not intermarry with them, because they will surely turn your hearts after their gods." Nevertheless, Solomon held fast to them in love.

1 KINGS 11:2

A mutual passion for live jazz. . .the home team. . .gourmet food. . .exotic travel bring a man and woman together. As they get to know each other, they discover they thoroughly enjoy each other's company. Their relationship moves from friendship to romance. So what's wrong with this picture? He is a Christian; she is not.

God instituted marriage as a way for a man and a woman to serve Him, but Christians and non-Christians serve different gods. Unbelievers and adherents of other faiths uphold values and principles often diametrically opposed to Christian values and principles. In marriage, whose beliefs will set the standard for the household? Whose ethics will win out in family matters and business dealings? As time passes and your spouse's influence rubs off on you, whom will you end up worshipping?

God forbade His Old Testament people Israel to marry nonbelievers, yet King Solomon let his desires trump his proverbial wisdom. For the sake of forging favorable treaties and establishing ties with other royal families, the king took many heathen wives and concubines into his household. The tolerant king let the ladies set up statues of their gods. Soon, Solomon himself included these gods in his worship of the true God. The entire country followed suit.

While interfaith marriages are not prohibited to Christians, we need to be aware of inherent challenges and pitfalls. We deprive ourselves of our spouse's spiritual support and his or her presence at worship. He or she cannot share in the religious upbringing of children without causing confusion to the children. A believing spouse can, however, be the way God uses to bring an unbeliever to faith. A Christian's daily witness through attitude, word, and action may lead an unbelieving spouse to know Jesus Christ.

No matter how many interests you and your beloved share, keep Christ in the picture. . .front and center. He makes all the difference.

Be encouraged and knit together by strong ties of love.
COLOSSIANS 2:2 NLT

THE WORLD SAYS:
"I can hang out with a 'bad' boy/girl now—when I get married, I'll find someone nice."

GOD SAYS:
"Bad company corrupts good morals."

Don't be fooled by those who say such things, for "bad company corrupts good character."

1 CORINTHIANS 15:33 NLT

In the past, the sexual exploits of a boy received a few smiles from the neighbors and the frank admiration of his friends. A girl daring to do the same thing called on herself a litany of unflattering epithets and a damaged reputation for life. Now, the former scenario rules for both boys and girls: Sexual experience is part of growing up (wink, wink). But when it comes time for marriage, both men and women look for someone with high standards, integrity, exemplary character, and who is meant for them alone!

Socially senseless, this pattern of behavior is rife with risks. Why would a godly man or woman choose as his or her life's companion someone who has, up until now, lived in a moral pigsty? What exactly do they have in common? If the person takes God's Word on sex so lightly, which other commandments will he or she be willing to break later on down the line? And why would a chaste person risk his or her physical health with someone who might pass on a sexually transmitted disease?

Spiritually stupid, "playing around" is anything but play. Dismissing God's clear commandment against sex outside of marriage offends God and insults the institution of marriage. Christians who do so subject their faith to ridicule and themselves to charges of hypocrisy. Their actions show they have no problem using others for their own selfish gratification. By being among the promiscuous, they put themselves under the influence of men and women who mock God, socializing with them, listening to their conversations, adopting their attitude toward life. Do you want that for yourself?

Sex is an intimate expression of love between husband and wife. No experience necessary—or desired. Believe in yourself and your future spouse enough to rest assured the two of you will figure out the physical aspect of marriage pretty quickly at the proper time.

If we confess our sins to him, he is faithful and just to forgive us and to cleanse us from every wrong.

1 JOHN 1:9 NLT

THE WORLD SAYS:
"Do unto others before they do unto you."

GOD SAYS:
"Do unto others as you would have them do unto you."

In everything, do to others what you would have them do to you.
MATTHEW 7:12

Wait for your future spouse. Wait for sex. Wait for. . .well, you're probably tired of waiting, so here's something you can do right away. No special situation is called for here. No minimum or maximum age limit. No dependence on anyone else, because the Golden Rule depends on you.

Jesus reiterated the Golden Rule near the end of a lengthy discourse called the Sermon on the Mount. In His sermon, Jesus described in detail God's expectations concerning our behavior toward one another. He summed up these teachings with the principle that we treat others the way we ourselves would like to be treated. Simple concept, but not easy to do!

By nature, we serve ourselves. If we think others might get something we want before we do, we grab first. If we suspect someone else might do us harm, we attack first. If another person offends us, we retaliate in kind—or worse. We subscribe to the battle-hardened, worldly principle: Watch out for Number One.

Jesus lays out a different principle—a Spirit-empowered, godly principle. If we're in Him, we act like Him. As God showers His goodness on the wicked and the righteous, so we shower His goodness on others in our relationships and interactions with others. As Christ came to save all people, so we serve everyone without regard to what they can do for us. On principle—God's principle—our service doesn't wait for a deserving person or the right conditions; nor is it put off until we feel like it. Our service happens whether or not the person we serve notices, cares, or ever says "thank you." We simply do what we'd like someone to do for us. We can, because Jesus has done everything for us already.

Start the Golden Rule of godly service to others with the next word you speak. . .the next action you take. No waiting!

"That is what the Son of Man has done: He came to serve, not be served—and then to give away his life in exchange for the many who are held hostage."

MATTHEW 20:28 MSG

THE WORLD SAYS:
"You can divorce your spouse on any grounds."

GOD SAYS:
"He who divorces his spouse on any grounds except unfaithfulness commits adultery."

[Jesus said,] "I tell you that anyone who divorces his wife, except for marital unfaithfulness, and marries another woman commits adultery."

MATTHEW 19:9

When you ask the wrong question, you'll get the wrong answer. If you ask, "Do I have grounds for divorce?" you will start cultivating those grounds. But if you ask, "Am I doing everything I can to build up and strengthen my marriage?" you will get a far different answer. And you will have asked the right question.

Because of sin—the world's sin, our sin—divorce is inevitable, even among Christians. In the hardness of our heart, we refuse to submit our lives to holiness. We allow selfishness to swallow generosity, accusation to stamp out admiration. Forgivable sins, yes, with sincere repentance and faith in Christ's sacrifice. Healable wounds, yes, in Christ's unconditional love. But an *avoidable* sin if the question of divorce never comes up.

Ask: "Am I doing everything I can to build up and strengthen my marriage?" Answer: I'm committed to my marriage and to my spouse. When trouble comes—and it will, as long as we live this side of heaven—I neither think nor say the word *divorce*. It's simply not an option I give myself.

Answer: I compliment my spouse with endearing words of praise and encouragement. I turn away from complaints and criticisms and turn to kindness, admiration, pride, and respect.

Answer: I readily forgive, and I humbly ask for and accept forgiveness. I keep no record of wrongs and offenses. I know the words "I'm sorry," and I'm strong enough to say them.

Answer: We worship together at home and in church. Together, we strengthen our faith, mature in the Christian life, and enjoy the fellowship of other disciples. In making Christ our priority and Him the center of our home, we build a bulwark against the forces of Satan, the world, and our own flesh.

Answer: In Him, yes. I'm doing everything I can to build up and strengthen my marriage.

"Because God created this organic union of the two sexes, no one should desecrate his art by cutting them apart."

MATTHEW 19:6 MSG

SEX.

THE WORLD SAYS:
"If she doesn't shape up, I'm outta here."

GOD SAYS:
"Mercy triumphs over judgment."

If someone is caught in a sin, you who are spiritual should restore him gently. But watch yourself, or you also may be tempted. Carry each other's burdens, and in this way you will fulfill the law of Christ.

GALATIANS 6:1–2

In the parable of the Good Samaritan, Jesus told of a traveler attacked by bandits and left to die at the side of the road. A priest and a temple assistant walked by. Both saw, but avoided, the wounded man. Then a Samaritan came along. The Samaritan traveler stopped, knelt down, soothed and bandaged the victim's wounds, took him to an inn, and paid for his care. (See Luke 10:30–37.)

Yes, we have a God-given responsibility to one another. When we see someone wounding himself in a sinful lifestyle, we aren't to pass on by so he can "do his own thing." Though others may avoid someone sidelined by addiction, depression, or illness, Jesus tells us to offer assistance. How much more when it's our loved one suffering under a crushing burden!

More important than the nature of the problem, though, is the nature of our help. To the sinner, we humbly articulate God's Law, fully aware of ourselves as sinners apt to fall into the very same sin, or worse. To the wounded, we patiently apply His Gospel, knowing ourselves as ones in need of God's loving promises. To all, with Spirit-empowered care, we treat the other person as one who is as beloved of God as ourselves.

While you were "by the side of the road" in sin, God valued you. He came to you with His firm and unchangeable Law. In its mirror, you saw how bad off you really were. He took you up in His arms and cleansed your wounds in the waters of holy baptism. He brought you to the shelter of faith, gave you a spirit of repentance, and robed you in His righteousness.

He took responsibility for you a long time ago. When you sin, He reaches out to you with the words, "I'm here to help." Who needs to hear those words from you today?

I'll make a list of GOD's gracious dealings, all the things GOD has done that need praising, all the generous bounties of GOD, his great goodness. . .compassion lavished, love extravagant.

ISAIAH 63:7 MSG

THE WORLD SAYS:
"I can't get no satisfaction."

GOD SAYS:
"Real satisfaction comes from Me."

*Death and Destruction are never satisfied,
and neither are the eyes of man.*
PROVERBS 27:20

Though the world promises you satisfaction, it doesn't want you to be satisfied. Why would it? Advertisers want you to keep buying their products and the latest upgrades. Retailers want you to keep trying on up-to-the-minute fashions and must-have accessories. Film studios want you to keep going to blockbuster movies and keep purchasing the licensed merchandise. In short, the world wants you to keep wanting.

Some Christians respond by shunning the world of commercialism and commerce. While such a path may be taken in pursuit of personal holiness and special service to the Lord, God doesn't command His people to opt out of consumerism altogether. But He does place in front of us certain rules and clear warnings about it. He cautions us, for example, against thinking the world can provide for us a sense of wholeness, purpose, value, or satisfaction.

The world can't and won't do it, but it never ceases to tease us with its promises. Okay, so we're smart enough to know a new top-of-the-line sports car won't bring contentment, but what about exciting, exhilarating experiences. . . say an exotic cruise or white-water rafting? You realize the lovey-dovey couple on screen are actors, but what if. . .what if. . .your partner looked as macho or as dazzling as they? Wouldn't you be more satisfied?

God preempts our sinful thoughts and ceaseless desires by saying, "I am your satisfaction. Find your contentment, your wholeness, in Me. Seek your purpose in following Me." When He is your complete satisfaction, the world's offers fall into place. You have the freedom not to need any of them, so you can choose any of them you want. *Any* you want? Sure. Because with Christ as your satisfaction, you aren't going to want anything harmful for you or others; anything outside or beyond the resources He has given you; anything that doesn't contribute to your wholesome, Christ-centered enjoyment of life.

"I'll make sure. . .that my people have more than enough."
JEREMIAH 31:14 MSG

THE WORLD SAYS:
"You may forgive, but you won't forget."

GOD SAYS:
"Forgive as I have forgiven you."

As far as the east is from the west, so far has he removed our transgressions from us.

PSALM 103:12

Someone who refuses to let go of the past is like Lot's wife. God directed Lot to take his family and leave their home in Sodom, as He intended to destroy the sin-filled, unrepentant cities of Sodom and Gomorrah. God commanded, "Run! And don't look back!" At some distance from Sodom, Lot's wife turned around. She became a pillar of salt.

When we "look back" at yesterday's hurts, offenses, and insults, we stand today as lifeless and static as a pillar of salt. Forever paralyzed by the past, we'll endlessly refresh the pain of a thoughtless remark. We'll constantly bring up our loved ones' blunders and slant every story to highlight the flaws of our family members and friends. We'll nurse each unfortunate event in our lives until we've become rigid with resentment, bitterness, accusations, and anger.

God might very well command us, "Run! And don't look back!" Gazing back at destruction caused by the sins of others against us only brings about our own ruin. While we may never forget the fact that certain sinful actions occurred, we must—and can *with God's help*—let go of the anger we feel against the sinner. Not only will we reclaim our emotional well-being, but we'll be doing what God does for us every time we go before His throne in repentance.

God through Jesus Christ forgives the sins of the penitent sinner. No matter how offensive those sins were to Him. . . no matter how deeply they angered Him. . .no matter how blatantly His commandments were broken. . .He takes them (and their penalty of eternal damnation) far away from us and casts them out of His sight. In an awesome show of His almighty power and His unreserved grace, He forgives. . .and He never looks back. . .for Jesus' sake.

In your relationships, are you looking back. . .or looking forward? Are you a pillar of salt. . .or a pillar of light?

You lifted the cloud of guilt from your people,
you put their sins far out of sight.
Psalm 85:2 msg

THE WORLD SAYS:
*"Love is finding
the right person."*

GOD SAYS:
*"Love is becoming
the right person."*

*You, brethren, have been called to liberty; only do not use liberty as
an opportunity for the flesh, but through love serve one another.*

GALATIANS 5:13 NKJV

What's the singles scene like where you live? Some cities fare better than others when surveys reveal the best areas for singles. Top cities usually boast a hopping nightlife with plenty of clubs and restaurants, in addition to an abundance of cultural events and art galleries. A city amenable to singles clearly must provide lots of occasions for single men and women to find each other.

The surveys may accurately pinpoint trendy metropolitan areas and regions with more single than married people, but they imply that love is all about you finding Mr. or Ms. Right. The pressure is on you to go out, scan the faces around you, and determine if anyone present attracts you. If this describes you, consider for a moment how much time and effort you put into *searching* for the right person. Now think what you would do differently if this same time and effort, energy and action, were channeled into your *becoming* the right person.

Christian discipleship urges us to concern ourselves more with what we're giving than what we're getting. If we start searching for a person with particular characteristics, we're focusing on what we stand to get if and when we find this person. On the other hand, if we cultivate the quality of servanthood, we're centered on what we can give the people we can and do meet. And when we're busy paying attention to the needs of others, we'll discover their interesting, attractive, and endearing qualities. We tend to "find" the qualities that matter—holiness, compassion, kindness, humility, contentedness, joy—only when we ourselves share those qualities with others.

The dating scene in your town or city may rank anywhere from top-notch to nonexistent. Either way, let God handle the responsibility of finding the right person for you. Meanwhile, you can serve everyone. . .because the Holy Spirit has found you.

Those who have served well gain an excellent standing.
1 TIMOTHY 3:13

SEX.

THE WORLD SAYS:
"Real love looks the other way."

GOD SAYS:
"Speak the truth in love."

[Speak] the truth in love, [that you] may grow up in all things into Him who is the head—Christ.
EPHESIANS 4:15 NKJV

"If you can't say something nice. . ." So we avoid saying things apt to upset someone else. We never state a negative observation but instead overlook or explain away obvious problems. Yet Christian love compels us to tell the truth, even when it isn't "nice." When it's uncomfortable or unpleasant. When it hurts. When it's hard. So God tells us how to tell the truth.

We're not to launch into sweeping generalizations, name-calling, and scolding. We're forbidden to use "the truth" as an excuse to assert our opinions and judgments. After all, we possess the truth only by God's grace through His Word and the work of the Holy Spirit. It doesn't make us superior but rather gives us a sacred responsibility. God says to us, "Tell the truth in love" (see Ephesians 4:15 MSG).

Empowered by His Spirit, we know His truth. When it's necessary to confront someone with His truth, we're armed with God's Word, not personal opinion. For example, we see a gap between what God says and what a person's behavior shows. We're citing observable facts backed by specific examples.

If we ourselves know the truth, we speak as one sinner to another sinner. And we know how Christ treats sinners—He invites them to repent. He forgives them. He builds them up in faith and guides them in His true and holy way. When they backslide, He pulls them back again. He tells the truth with love—love that took Him all the way to the cross of Calvary. A Christlike willingness to tell the truth can be nothing less than a Christlike willingness to speak in love.

As Christian sons, daughters, spouses, mothers, fathers, aunts, uncles, and friends, we're called upon to be more than "nice." We're required to address tough issues with clarity and compassion. The Holy Spirit gives us the power—and the responsibility—to tell the truth in love.

Guide me in your truth and teach me.
PSALM 25:5

THE WORLD SAYS:
"Be nice to your spouse only if he/she is nice to you."

GOD SAYS:
"Be kind and tenderhearted to one another."

Be kind and compassionate to one another, forgiving each other, just as in Christ God forgave you.
EPHESIANS 4:32

From an early age, we figure out that some people treat us very well while others barely acknowledge our existence. A few may even cause us harm or injury. It's only natural, then, to develop a repertoire of reactions to people, depending on how they deal with us. Loving people get hugs and smiles. Indifferent people get dismissed. Mean people get a scowl or worse. We give what we get. It's a tit-for-tat world.

The world's Creator, however, works differently. He loves without first taking stock of what He stands to get in return. For example, He loved you before you were born—before you ever did anything, much less something nice. He sent His Son to pay for your sins, whether or not you ever remember to say "thank you" or regard His sacrifice with gratitude. He loves you right now, despite the fact there's nothing you ever did or can do to earn His love. He loves you no matter what kind of life you have led, or the sins and weaknesses you struggle with now. He'll love you in the future, even if you fail to live up to His will for your life. Tit-for-tat? Thank goodness—thank God!—no.

Christlike love doesn't follow love, it leads with love. It's not dependent on the reactions of others around you, but it comes from the Spirit's work within you. Christlike love doesn't get offended and walk away when it's not recognized by others, nor does it get puffed up and prideful when it's praised. It's a simple constant. . .as constant as God's love for you.

In your relationships, lead with love. Where others withhold love, you can be the first to give love. Where others give love, add to it with rejoicing and praise for the One who is love: God.

"You understand and know me. I'm GOD, and I act in loyal love. I do what's right and set things right and fair, and delight in those who do the same things."
JEREMIAH 9:24 MSG

THE WORLD SAYS:
"If your spouse gets angry and screams at you, scream back."

GOD SAYS:
"A soft answer turns away wrath."

A gentle answer turns away wrath, but a harsh word stirs up anger.
PROVERBS 15:1

If you want a bigger and hotter campfire, just add fuel to it. If you want a fire to consume the forest, leave it alone and let it ignite the surrounding trees, sticks, and bushes. The same holds true with anger.

Anger thrives on fuel. As long as it's fed with raging words, it grows bigger and hotter. Throw heightened emotions and elevated levels of abusive speech into it, and its fury increases even more rapidly. Without clear boundaries, anger consumes more territory as sparks ignite past grievances, unsettled differences, and old hurts. Even when the words stop, anger smolders under the debris of charred relationships and the damage of words that should never have been spoken.

Sure, it's tempting to "meet fire with fire," but the blazing flame of anger is better met—and spiritually met—with the soft answer of Christian fellowship. A person caught up in anger's passion needs kindness, not another reason to get angry. As with a campfire you want to put out, clear the kindling—your own angry reaction, your judgment as to the justification of the anger, your discomfort. Once the person's anger subsides, cover it with your forgiveness. Allow it no hidden life by holding a grudge or planning your rebuttal. As far as you're able to do so, assist a chronically angry person in finding healthy ways to deal with the cause of his or her anger. Pray not only with, but for the person as well. The fire of anger burns us, but it consumes the angry person.

Anger destroys lives when it becomes a habitual way of reacting to annoyances and frustrations, when it bars productive communication, when it leaves indelible scars on relationships. But anger does not have to have the last word. Even from the scorched soil of a burned forest, new life blossoms.

Gracious speech is like clover honey—good taste to the soul, quick energy for the body.
PROVERBS 16:24 MSG

THE WORLD SAYS:
*"It's my way or
the highway."*

GOD SAYS:
*"Love does not insist on its
own way."*

[Love] is not self-seeking.
1 CORINTHIANS 13:5

Social activist and former first lady Eleanor Roosevelt once said, "More people are ruined by victory, I imagine, than by defeat." Indeed, there's small victory when we insist on getting our own way. In myopic pursuit of our own vision of what life should look like, we blind ourselves to all it has to offer.

If by personal charisma or conferred authority we succeed in forcing others to submit to us, we're likely to start considering our opinions indispensable to the functioning of our marriage, household, or business. Controlling behavior clouds our relationships, because family, friends, and coworkers quickly realize that nothing they say or any idea they contribute will change or challenge our one-track mind.

If we always get our own way, we're not given to gratitude for what we have—just the opposite. We think we've earned it all by our superior insights and strong management. When by reason of a reversal of fortunes, diminished status, illness, or advanced age we lose our influence over people and events, our world crumbles quickly. Sooner or later, the "victory" of getting our own way works to our own defeat.

God's love, nourished in us by His Spirit, gives us another way—His way. His love in us through the gift of the Holy Spirit invites us to put others first. His love listens to and acknowledges the needs and concerns of others. It values other people and welcomes their perspectives and ideas. His love allows us to work with others productively. His love makes us want to go along with someone else's way of doing things just for the pleasure of it. His love accepts whatever life brings, because it sees opportunities, gifts, and hidden blessings in all things.

People notice love's leadership. Ironically, though love never insists on its own way, people are drawn to follow the way of love.

Don't push your way to the front; don't sweet-talk your way to the top. Put yourself aside, and help others get ahead.
PHILIPPIANS 2:3 MSG

THE WORLD SAYS:
"Get even."

GOD SAYS:
"Love does not keep a record of wrongs."

Live at peace with everyone. Do not take revenge, my friends.
ROMANS 12:18–19

At work, it's considered a bad career move to haughtily huff, "That's not my job!" when asked to perform a task. But when ill treatment or hurt feelings tempt us to take revenge on someone, we can—with God's approval—confidently declare, "That's not my job." God has reserved revenge for Himself. As long as it's possible to do so without diluting or disobeying God's Word, we're to live peaceably with our spouse, relatives, friends, fellow church members, coworkers. . .even with our enemies. . .even when they say and do hurtful things.

God asks us to act so counterintuitively because He acts just that way toward us. Despite our long record of wrongs against Him and His commandments, He takes no retaliatory measures against us. Instead, God sent His Son Jesus to bear the punishment of our sins so we could wear the purity of His perfect life and glorious resurrection. He forgives us completely, so likewise, we're to forgive others.

Does this mean Christians are the world's doormat? No. It means our willingness to forgive rather than retaliate models Christ's dealings with us. It means we set standards of behavior and personal boundaries not out of fear, vengeance, or defensiveness, but out of sacred respect for God in us and in others. Such godly actions witness to His love for us, and our example serves to bring others to the knowledge of salvation in Jesus Christ.

Not by your own willpower, but by His "cross-power," you can turn away from vengeance. His Spirit at work in your life lifts your eyes from hurt feelings, real and perceived grievances, and instances of ill-treatment and focuses them on His cross. In the knowledge of your own forgiveness, you have the power to live by His Word. You have the means to forgive your enemies. And because He gives it to you, it's your job. . . and your privilege.

Don't let evil get the best of you, but conquer evil by doing good.
Romans 12:21 nlt

THE WORLD SAYS:
"Staying in love requires good sex."

GOD SAYS:
"Sex is not the foundation of love; it's the expression of love."

The wife's body does not belong to her alone but also to her husband. In the same way, the husband's body does not belong to him alone but also to his wife.

1 CORINTHIANS 7:4

Take a ride in a time machine back to first-century Corinth, and you'll find yourself in familiar cultural territory. A cosmopolitan port city, Corinth welcomed tourists, traders, and travelers from all parts of the known world. Rampant immorality followed in the wake of financial fortunes, idle shipmen, affluent visitors, and lavish luxuries. Inevitably—as it does today—the morals of the city seeped into the Christian church.

While some Corinthian Christians went along with the sexual standards of the day, others headed in the other direction. They wondered if sex was bad and would be best avoided altogether, even in marriage. In his letter to them, Paul gave an explicit, XXX-rated response: Married Christians can look forward to good sex!

God created the sexual inclination of man and woman. He instituted marriage, giving a husband claim to his wife's body and a wife claim to her husband's body within the bonds of holy matrimony. Love shared between husband and wife compels them to give up their individual rights for the sake of the other. In marriage, neither husband nor wife has the right to arbitrarily or capriciously abstain from sex.

Love shared between husband and wife also compels them to claim each other in a spirit of care, concern, and appreciation for the other. They can have good sex because what they do is an expression of love, not a show of force, power, or dominance. It's an occasion of comfortable pleasure for both, not an excuse to inflict physical or emotional hurt. It's an act of intimate, loving union, not a function of selfish gratification.

The secular world calls anything consenting adults want to do "good" sex. Some Christians react by deciding all sex is "bad" sex. God's Word supports neither view. Sex is good because God created it, and He instructs us to keep it "good" in the comfort and security of marriage.

[Avoid] a life shaped by things and feelings instead of by God.
COLOSSIANS 3:5 MSG

THE WORLD SAYS:
"Real love is about getting your needs met."

GOD SAYS:
"Real love is about meeting your spouse's needs."

Unless the LORD builds the house, they labor in vain who build it; unless the LORD guards the city, the watchman stays awake in vain.

PSALM 127:1 NKJV

Question: How do you know when the world is lying about marriage? Answer: Whenever it's talking about marriage. Pick up a magazine and read articles purporting to tell you how to get what you want from your marriage. Watch movies and sitcoms for examples of couples struggling to maintain their "identity" in marriage. Listen to your friends talk about what they want in a spouse: hot body, prestigious career, lots of money. . .and a sense of independence so she won't be responsible for his needs, nor he responsible for her needs. Rest assured you're reading, seeing, and hearing lies.

The world tells lies about marriage because it long ago ceased to hear God tell the truth about marriage. God describes marriage as a lifelong holy union for one man and one woman. He blesses married couples with the sacred privilege of physical intimacy and the gift of children. He directs husbands and wives to live in mutual love, honor, helpfulness, and faithfulness. Of course, doing so isn't always fun or easy. It means sacrifice sometimes, so the world turns away at this point in pursuit of more immediate, more sensual pleasures.

God has something truly sublime in mind when He calls a married couple one body, one flesh. Husbands and wives who insist on doing their "own thing" miss their God-given opportunity to live for something besides their own self-gratification. They may never discover or appreciate the worth of anyone beyond that person's usefulness to him or her at the moment. Marriage, entered into for selfish reasons and lived in pursuit of selfish goals, is like a fantasy castle in a fairy tale. You can talk about it all you want to, but it isn't real.

How do you know when you're hearing the truth about marriage? When you're listening to the Word of Truth.

[Love] isn't always "me first."
1 CORINTHIANS 13:5 MSG

THE WORLD SAYS:
"Divorce is the best option when love grows cold."

GOD SAYS:
"Rekindling love by your words and your actions is the best option when love grows cold."

[Love] believes all things [and] hopes all things.
1 CORINTHIANS 13:7 NKJV

According to legend, the Vikings introduced the English to mead, or honey wine, also called "love potion." A tradition emerged among newly wedded English couples to drink honey wine during the first month of their marriage, "from moon to moon." Thus the word *honeymoon*.

Some couples today seem to expect the honey wine and the honeymoon to last forever. When the honeymoon's bliss and the honey wine's savor fade, they toss out the empty bottle—and their spouse—and go in search of someone else. Unable to imagine love without the ecstatic feelings and euphoric excitement of the honeymoon, they decide love no longer resides in their marriage. How wrong!

Christians can go through life—and enter marriage— with a more realistic attitude, based on biblical wisdom. While they still accept their blessings with joy and gratitude, they can also expect to share in life's trials, troubles, and sorrows. But Christian couples need not fear loss, because they can trust and rely on God's help, comfort, and strength when things get tough. They realize, with Spirit-given wisdom, that God uses adverse circumstances to bring new life, new growth, new maturity to individuals. . .and to relationships.

Neither the honey wine nor the honeymoon will last forever—and that's okay. Why? Because love isn't something meted out by measure, and when you've used your allotted amount, you're out of it. The sum of love isn't contained in the feelings and passions of one particular moment. Real love presses on despite feelings and endures despite circumstances. It cultivates deep roots and bears sweet, ripe fruit with time.

If you think the honey wine was used up long ago, consider it your invitation to a deeper, richer, more mature relationship. Use it as a God-given challenge to renovate, revive, revisit, and rediscover love with your spouse. In your marriage, you two have all the ingredients you need to mix up a sweet new "love potion"!

Love never dies.
1 CORINTHIANS 13:8 MSG

THE WORLD SAYS:
"It's okay to keep secrets from your spouse."

GOD SAYS:
"Honesty and transparency contribute to intimacy."

Therefore each of you must put off falsehood and speak truthfully to his neighbor, for we are all members of one body.

EPHESIANS 4:25

Christopher Columbus, on his first venture west, kept two logs. In one—the one he kept secret—he recorded what he believed were accurate notes of distances traveled. In the other—the one he shared with the crew—he shortened the distances so the sailors would feel comfortably close to home.

We deceive others for various reasons. Sometimes it's because we think they can't handle the truth. Because we're ashamed to admit the truth. Because we like having a private life few people know about. When we keep secrets for any reason, however, we're sailing in dangerous waters.

Secrets shipwreck love. If you keep secrets, you're not giving yourself completely to your relationship. You enslave yourself, for you have to keep vigilant guard over your secrets. When—not if, but when—your secrets come to light, your spouse wonders what else you've kept hidden. Christ invites repentance of all sins, including ones as serious as this one. Your new life in Him will strengthen you to live openly and honestly in all your relationships, as well as deal with the consequences of past behavior.

If you have been deceived by your spouse, you have been sinned against in a painful way. Most likely, your ability to trust him or her again with your affection, your intimacy, your love has been deeply damaged. Forgiveness in the face of such a betrayal is a challenge, and you would be well-advised to seek the counsel of your pastor or a mature Christian friend or fellow church member. Take heart in God's power and willingness to heal your wounds and help you live again in a healthy and wholesome intimate relationship.

As a postscript to Columbus's sly plan to cover up the truth, it turned out that the "false" log proved more accurate than the "true" one. So the deceiver ended up being the one most deceived!

[Love] takes pleasure in the flowering of truth.
1 CORINTHIANS 13:6 MSG

THE WORLD SAYS:
"Cupid is the author of love."

GOD SAYS:
"I am the Author and Foundation of love."

Those who live according to the sinful nature have their minds set on what that nature desires; but those who live in accordance with the Spirit have their minds set on what the Spirit desires.

ROMANS 8:5

In Roman mythology, Cupid is the son of Venus, the goddess of love. In some stories, he's a dashing young man who woos the lovely princess Psyche. In others, he's an impish boy who shoots love darts at gods and humans alike. Artists portray Cupid as a chubby, winged infant with remarkable archery skills. Nicked by an arrow of his, you're in love.

The world may not claim that cherubic infants inflict love stabs with well-aimed darts, but it speaks as if there's some truth to the story. After all, when love strikes, it strikes, right? You can't help it. Furthermore, you have to act on it or you're repressed. . .relegated to an unfulfilled life. . .condemned to misery.

God, the true Author of love, differentiates between love and lust. Love, rooted in His Spirit, loves in obedience to His will. Lust, fixed in human flesh, lusts after things of the flesh. Love proves strong, faithful, and long-lasting. Lust flees after it has possessed and used the object of its desire. Love stays through all circumstances, while lust leaves at its own convenience.

You can tell the difference between true love and fleshly lust. Look at the actions it suggests—godly actions or sinful actions? Check out its quality—pure, lasting quality or impure, transitory quality? Look at the attitude it creates—thanksgiving to God for sending such a wonderful person into your life, or shame in His presence because you desire what is not yours?

If you see a gap between what God calls love and what you're feeling, step back from the relationship and squarely into your relationship with Him. Your heavenly Father can help you let go of wrongful desires. . .all you need to do is ask in a spirit of sincerity and repentance.

Let Cupid have his day—it's on February 14 each year. Let the Spirit have your heart—now and forever.

[Don't give in to] impurity, lust, doing whatever you feel like whenever you feel like it.

COLOSSIANS 3:5 MSG

THE WORLD SAYS:
"A good book on physical love will help your sex life."

GOD SAYS:
"Sacrificial love will help your sex life."

My help comes from the LORD, who made the heavens and the earth!

PSALM 121:2 NLT

Sex proved disappointing for both. Neither found much pleasure in it, but neither wanted to be the first to say anything. Instead, he brought home an erotic magazine and invited her to look through it with him. Meanwhile, she recommended to him a romantic novel she had just enjoyed.

If the couple had gone to God's Word, they would have found much more than a temporary fix for their problem. Christian couples who share God's Word share one source of information. Rather than nursing contradictory his-and-her concepts of what romance looks like, they read and discuss together one truth for all times.

Sex books, romantic novels, and erotic magazines promote the salacious aspects of sex and often paint an unrealistic—if not perverted—picture of what sex means. If followed, they force couples into roles designed to gratify carnal fantasies. In God's Word, the married Christian couple finds that sexual expression flows from the spiritual reality of selfless love, mutual honor, and compassionate acceptance. Husband and wife find lasting satisfaction in accepting each other as a blessing from the Lord, in pleasing each other, and in discovering together what constitutes the physical aspects of their sex life.

Are you and your spouse looking for help with your sex life? Start by looking in the right place. Prayerfully examine your desires and expectations in the light of God's Word. Are you focused on what you should get—or what you can give? Do you merely want to master sexual techniques—or are you open to patiently discovering sexual pleasure with your spouse? Do you think of sex in images gleaned from books and magazines—or in images of Christ's sacrificial and all-encompassing love for you?

For help with your sex life, go ahead and pick up a book. Just make sure it's the one Book with the right answers!

*Let the Word of Christ—the Message—have the run of the house.
Give it plenty of room in your lives.*
COLOSSIANS 3:16 MSG

SEX.

THE WORLD SAYS:
"Attraction is instant."

GOD SAYS:
"Intimacy takes time."

God bought you with a high price. So you must honor God with your body.

1 Corinthians 6:20 NLT

He meets her eyes across a crowded room. She smiles. Next scene, they're bouncing around in bed together. And why not? In the movies, the couple has two hours tops to say hello, overcome various obstacles, get down to business, and deal with the consequences! Life, however, requires a longer attention span.

Instant attraction is thrilling. How electrifying to feel suddenly smitten! How flattering to attract such unexpected attention! It very well could be the beginning of something serious. But rushing from attraction to attachment brings long-term—if not lifelong—consequences. False and deceitful suitors move quickly to capture our first thought because they don't want to risk our second thoughts. They know that having sex now forges emotional bonds, which they can exploit later to our disadvantage. They know effusive flattery, lavish gifts, and emotional attachment blind us to danger signals we would note in less intense, less hurried, circumstances.

Giving in to instant attraction usually comes to a sad end. Passionate encounters may bring an unintended or unwanted pregnancy before either party is prepared for parenting. Marriage before members of the couple really know each other invites the risk of marrying the wrong person. After an overheated rush to secure marital privileges, one or both may realize they weren't at all ready for marital responsibilities. Regrets, divorce, single parenthood, unhappy memories—just a few of the enduring results of instant courtships.

God gave you your life. . .you are precious to Him. Marriage means you will share with and give to your spouse the gift of your life. You have a responsibility to yourself and to your boyfriend or girlfriend to let God's path be known to both of you. The bonds of friendship and faith, of love and intimacy, take time. . .and will also stand the test of time. You're God's gift to your spouse. . .and you're certainly worth the wait.

[Don't just grab] whatever attracts your fancy.
Colossians 3:5 msg

THE WORLD SAYS:
"If you meet someone you like better than your spouse, go for it."

GOD SAYS:
"Love is faithful."

Your love, O LORD, reaches to the heavens, your faithfulness to the skies.
PSALM 36:5

She gained twenty-five pounds since their wedding day. After all, they enjoyed cooking and eating together. Her stylized, colored hair grew back to its natural brown. With two small children, she had no time or money left to visit the beauty salon. Managing the children was difficult, and she sometimes became irritable. And those homemade meals were reduced to what could be easily microwaved. All this didn't go unnoticed by her husband. Despite the many blessings in their lives, he was ready to walk out the door to the arms of his younger, thinner, more carefree secretary.

How tragic when people make choices, letting the pressures of life push a marriage partner out the door. After all, a newer partner has his or her own set of problems. At least an original partner has predictable foibles. Don't the words "Till death do you part" equal lifelong faithfulness?

Vows reading "for richer, for poorer; in sickness and in heath," also demand stick-to-itiveness in marriage.

When somebody says they fell out of love with their original partner or they met someone they like better, they are oftentimes saying there is less responsibility with another person.

Commitment is more than grit-teethed determination. Commitment is discovering what pleases your partner and giving to them. When you give to them, they are likely to give back to you. When a couple decides to live by this practice, they add glue to their vows and open up a lifetime of mutual pleasing and satisfaction. Life's pressures can dampen fun and frolic, it's true. But when you stick to the vows, laugh despite the pains, and hold onto your "old paint," you'll together form a bond that pleases God and, in the long run, will please you, too.

[Love] keeps going to the end.
1 CORINTHIANS 13:7 MSG

THE WORLD SAYS:
"A one-night stand is exciting."

GOD SAYS:
"A lifetime of commitment is fulfilling."

The Lord appeared to us in the past, saying: "I have loved you with an everlasting love; I have drawn you with loving-kindness."
Jeremiah 31:3

A reporter asked a famous Hollywood actor, "What's it like to have a beautiful woman every night?" The actor answered frankly. "It stinks. I wish I could wake up every morning to somebody I loved." This honest man traded nightly pleasures for daily pain and frustration.

He and all who practice one-night stands face exhausting obstacles. Whenever they want to have one, they have to "go on the hunt" requiring emotional and physical energy. They wake up next to someone they hardly know. They might not even remember their partner's name. These one-night stands offer sex but not love.

Think about the moments of love that partners share in lifelong marriage. Newlyweds thrill with great expectations for their future. They marvel at the arrival of children, knowing they cocreated life. As the children grow, they find satisfaction in teaching them the ropes of life. Even childless couples find fulfillment in blessing God side by side, serving God through serving others. As empty-nesters, they can finally do some of the things they've always wanted to do, or they can start new careers or service projects. Finally, as golden-agers, they can quietly cherish the memories of their past glory days.

In a lifetime marriage, sex takes on a different role, too. It becomes an expression of mutual love instead of just an act of pleasure. When you learn what pleases your lifelong partner, you can "make love" all day long through simple, loving acts like a hug or a pat on the back. By building love during the day, your sex at night can be more fulfilling. Plus, you'll wake up the next morning beside someone you love and get to do it all over again that day!

[Kill] off everything connected with [the] way of death:
sexual promiscuity.
COLOSSIANS 3:5 MSG

THE WORLD SAYS:
"I can't wait."

GOD SAYS:
"Real love is willing to wait."

Daughters of Jerusalem, I charge you: Do not arouse or awaken love until it so desires.

SONG OF SOLOMON 8:4

The unmarried man in his late thirties began to worry. He felt like he needed to find a wife right away. So on his dates, he tried to rush things along a little. He often appeared too anxious, too attentive, and too willing to please. Even after first dates, he would move in for a kiss. Women turned their heads and said goodnight. These women wanted a friend that might develop into something more, but all he wanted was instant intimacy, and he never found it.

Both men and women can try to "awaken love before it so desires." The bold sinner can find easy sex out in the rough-and-tumble world of barroom hookups. The more discriminating "love-pusher" operates like the above male lonely heart. Either way, God doesn't want you to relate to the opposite sex out of a position of weakness and fear. He longs to use you to bless each other and regard each other as brothers and sisters, regardless of the romantic outcome.

First Corinthians 13:4 says "love is patient." It's hard to believe that when the object of your love doesn't really pay you proper attention. Task-oriented people want to see results. They want to see the relationship "in the bag." But perhaps God has other plans for your relationships. Perhaps God wants to teach you forbearance. Perhaps God wants to teach you how to really talk with members of the opposite sex. Or, maybe He wants to keep you single right now in order to use you in ways you couldn't if you were married or attached. Regardless of the reason for your singleness or loneliness, God loves you and wants to use all circumstances to help shape you into holiness and righteousness.

Be. . .content.

Colossians 3:13 msg

THE WORLD SAYS:
*"Lust contributes
to great sex."*

GOD SAYS:
*"Loving-kindness contributes
to great sex."*

*Put to death, therefore, whatever belongs to your earthly nature:
sexual immorality, impurity, lust, evil desires and greed, which is
idolatry.*

COLOSSIANS 3:5

Hal couldn't understand why his wife wasn't as adventurous and spontaneous as she used to be. He thought she enjoyed it when he would come home from work at odd hours to have sex. He thought she liked duplicating some of the bizarre stuff he had seen from a pornographic film. She, in fact, did not. She had only obliged him in the early part of their marriage to make him happy. Now his lust was making her frustrated. She felt like a piece of meat that needed to perform on demand to his cravings. She couldn't remember the last time he had asked her how and when she wanted sex. Meanwhile, her own heart grew cold toward him as her romantic needs fizzled. Hal's lust was driving them apart.

Lust says, "I must get my own way. Right now. . .in this manner." It might even say, "Join me in this perverse act." Loving-kindness says, "Let's do this right." It respects the other person and his or her needs. It says, "Let's discuss what pleases each other." It might even say, "I'll put my own wishes aside for now to please you."

You'll never know what your partner considers great sex unless you talk about it before passion heats up. Great sex involves good listening, patience, and restraint. It might even involve nonsexual things like taking out the garbage and doing kind acts for one another. When both partners feel valued and appreciated, it's easier to reflect that love for each other in the bedroom. When all systems are go and both parties understand each other, then passion can really fire up. Through good communication, patience, and submitting to one another in love, both partners can find their needs (and even desires) fulfilled.

[Love] doesn't force itself on others.

1 Corinthians 13:5 msg

THE WORLD SAYS:
"Love is blind."

GOD SAYS:
"Love sees but accepts anyway."

"You will know the truth, and the truth will set you free."

JOHN 8:32

Sherry thought, *Maybe I had it coming.* Her boyfriend, Ron, had backhanded her hard across the mouth. In weeks to come, Ron slapped Sherry regularly. She tolerated it because she had aways thought, *Love is blind. I can overlook his anger.* This kind of blind love should never happen.

God's Word says, "Love your neighbor as yourself" (Matthew 22:39). There is no love involved by enduring damage and shame. It's impossible to love yourself and allow yourself to be battered and abused.

This kind of blind love sees no need for improvement. It ignores danger signs. It even puts its practitioners at risk for physical or emotional trauma. It eventually collapses under the weight of its own sinful practices.

True love, however, sees the reality of things and offers love at the appropriate distance. It accepts the person but hates the sin—such as physical or emotional abuse. It seeks help and patiently awaits improving physical, emotional, and spiritual health. True love also recognizes improvement and picks its battles carefully. After all, there's a huge difference between physical abuse in a relationship and a man who merely forgets to put the toilet seat down after using it. These minor problems demand lots of patience and mercy. True love sees these minor foibles but doesn't withhold love because of them.

If the truth sets you free, you need to have your eyes and ears open enough to see the truth. Recognize the realities of your situation. Know that God loves you both and has a solution for your dilemmas. He is your answer. He is your solution. When you accept Him into your heart, claim your old nature as dead, lean on Him to lead and guide you to new territory, and stake your claim as a new creation, you are well on your way.

When you're in over your head, I'll be there with you. When you're in rough waters, you will not go down.
Isaiah 43:2 MSG

THE WORLD SAYS:
"Love is never having to say, 'I'm sorry.'"

GOD SAYS:
"Real love is being willing to say, 'I'm sorry.'"

"Stop judging others, and you will not be judged.
Stop criticizing others, or it will all come back on you.
If you forgive others, you will be forgiven."

LUKE 6:37 NLT

Capturing the attention of a generation, film fans recall one memorable line from the 1970 movie *Love Story*: "Love means never having to say you're sorry." The line was uttered by Ali MacGraw as a dying Radcliffe music student named Jenny Cavilleri. The statement sounds convincing, but really it doesn't endure close scrutiny. In reality, love requires forgiveness and reconciliation. Human beings sin against God and each other. It's our nature, and it's inevitable. Without the words "I'm sorry," we're doomed to be separated from each other in wounded loneliness.

The words "I'm sorry" represent first aid to broken relationships. Think about the last time you hurt your spouse. Did you ignore the problem and hope it would go away? Or did you talk about it and admit your share of the damage you created over the issue?

Being willing to say you're sorry isn't easy. It takes guts. No one wants to admit fault. But recognition of a problem is the first step in overcoming it. If you stuff it and say you did nothing wrong, then you are at an impasse. You can't achieve progress because you can't admit you are heading in the wrong direction. Don't wait for your partner to admit their share of the blame. Perhaps they need your courageous lead. When they see you admit your sin, they'll be more likely to examine their own hearts and admit theirs. If you have both given your lives to Christ and have received His Spirit, forgiveness should be a normal expression of your character.

If you haven't received Christ yet, reach out to Him and ask for strength to forgive. When you forgive each other and love deeply, this will cover a multitude of sins.

Be. . .quick to forgive an offense. Forgive as quickly and completely as the Master forgave you.

Colossians 3:13 msg

THE WORLD SAYS:
"I'll love you if you love me."

GOD SAYS:
"I'll love you even when you don't love Me."

God demonstrates his own love for us in this: While we were still sinners, Christ died for us.

ROMANS 5:8

The young man married his sweetheart, even though she was dying of cancer. He knew that soon she wouldn't be able to talk to him or hug him back. He knew her personality would also deteriorate. He didn't care. He loved her. He wanted to love her until she died. Another wife married a happy, giving man, only to see his behavior change after their wedding day. He neglected her and denied her faith. At first, she nagged him to come around, but then she decided to pray and serve him unconditionally. Months turned into years, but without saying a word, she never gave up on him, and eventually, her dedication to him (contrasted with the harsh, cruel world he saw around him) softened and changed his heart.

God set the ultimate example for unconditional love. He looked down on earth and saw what a sorry job we were doing of loving Him and each other. We were stinky, rotten, filthy sinners. We were clueless, walking dead men, unable to know or receive any love. Yet, in His mercy, God sent His Son, Jesus, down to earth. Here, Jesus loved, healed, and fed all: loveable and unlovable. In fact, He was known as a "Friend of sinners." Then at the proper time, He demonstrated His ultimate act of love by taking the blame and punishment for our sin. He laid down His life in the greatest sacrificial gesture ever recorded in human history. He paid the price for our sins—yours and mine.

Are you willing to show love to your spouse, even to the point of death? Even when they don't deserve it? Even if they don't love you back? Unconditional love is the greatest power the earth has ever known.

Pure grace and nothing but grace be with all who love.
EPHESIANS 6:24 MSG

SEX.

THE WORLD SAYS:
"Sex is the only thing."

GOD SAYS:
"Love is the real thing."

*There are three things that will endure—faith, hope, and love—
and the greatest of these is love.*

1 CORINTHIANS 13:13 NLT

Remember what Grandma used to say? "Everything in moderation." Turns out you *can* have too much of a good thing. Too much sunshine gives you skin cancer. Too many sweets rot your teeth and make you fat. And too much sex throws your priorities all out of line. Sure, regular sex can and should occur between two married people committed to each other. But when sex is elevated beyond its natural place, it transforms a beautiful expression of love into a habitual, sinful burden.

There is only one thing we shouldn't moderately do: love. We need to always love, because God always loves. He's always reaching out and always practicing the kinds of things we humans fail to achieve with one another. He's infinitely patient, infinitely kind, and infinitely serving.

We humans can love that kind of way because God made a way so He can live and love inside of us. Paul explains this phenomenon in Galatians. "I have been crucified with Christ and I no longer live, but Christ lives in me. The life I live in the body, I live by faith in the Son of God, who loved me and gave himself for me" (2:20). Since Christ now lives in us, we have the power and ability to reflect Christ's love to others. And this is a kind of love that will endure long after our physical bodies give out.

Before the first sex act occurred between Adam and Eve, God poured out His love among His Son and the angels, and then toward Adam. Love existed before sex, and it'll be around long after the end of time. When you recognize that love is greater than sex, then your sex will be greatly filled with love.

I'm bankrupt without love.

1 CORINTHIANS 13:3 MSG

THE WORLD SAYS:
"Dressing promiscuously will attract men."

GOD SAYS:
"Having inner beauty will attract the right man."

Your beauty should not come from outward adornment, such as braided hair and the wearing of gold jewelry and fine clothes. Instead, it should be that of your inner self, the unfading beauty of a gentle and quiet spirit, which is of great worth in God's sight.

1 PETER 3:3–4

Modesty isn't a word that is used very often these days. *Suggestive*, *revealing*, and *sexy* are the adjectives used to describe today's fashions. God has made a woman's body beautiful. But her beauty was designed to "intoxicate" only one man—her husband.

Ladies, you have a power of which you might not even be aware. You have allure. This power must be wielded with wisdom and righteousness. Immodesty creates casual arousal in men and misses the mark of God's intended plan for you.

Think about this. Perceived value increases worth. If you look cheap and easy, others will place that value on you. If you practice modesty, you tell others you think highly of yourself and you want to be treated with respect. Immodesty invites a guy to get a cheap thrill with no investment.

Modesty invites a guy to earn your virtue. Modesty may be a slower pace toward marriage and sex, but it's also sweeter. It invites romance. Men don't want the brazen hussy for a wife. They might look at them, call them, date them, and even have sex with them, but when it comes time to settle down, they say they want someone like "dear old mom."

Your modesty will allow your inner beauty to shine forth. If guys are too busy looking at the outside, they can't see your inside. A guy yearns for what he cannot have. A man of character will desire a woman who has control over her physical appearance and lets her inner beauty radiate.

When it's a part of your own body. . .you give it dignity and honor.
1 CORINTHIANS 12:23 MSG

THE WORLD SAYS:
"Everybody's doing it (having sex)."

GOD SAYS:
"Life is not dictated by what everybody does. You follow Me."

Jesus said to his disciples, "If anyone would come after me, he must deny himself and take up his cross and follow me."
MATTHEW 16:24

It was her defense when her father found a condom in her purse. The teenager pleaded, "Everybody's doing it. Everybody's having sex." Unimpressed, the father said, "What if everybody drank alcohol and then drove their car? What if everybody decided to jump off a cliff? Would you still do it then?" The youth had no response.

It has been said, to be truly great, observe the masses and do the opposite. Popularity does not equal benefit. Promiscuous young people could do well to learn from their formerly promiscuous elders. Formerly promiscuous people often admit their present regret and pain. They compare current spouses to past lovers. They understand strong temptation to ditch current spouses because it was their common practice. Only those set free from their pasts, by the grace of God, find the strength to keep a renewed, clean heart.

Scripture readers and followers know God has the final say on this matter. From Genesis through the Levitical law on up through the Gospels and Epistles, the entire Bible points to the standard of "no sex until marriage and faithfulness within marriage." God's say-so makes no provision for "Everybody's doing it; therefore it must be okay."

God's not a stern taskmaster, trying to steal away our fun. He knows that His way offers us the greatest chance for emotional, spiritual, and physical health. Premarital sex carries many risks.

In fact, Christ knows about strong temptation—in all areas of life, including the area of sexuality. Yet He lived a celibate life. His short ministry on earth demanded singleness of purpose and marital status. Though we don't all have to share in His celibacy, His disciplined way of life offers the greatest chance for health and holiness.

Be prepared. You're up against far more than you can handle on your own. Take all the help you can get, every weapon God has issued, so that when it's all over but the shouting you'll still be on your feet.

EPHESIANS 6:13 MSG

THE WORLD SAYS:
"Give up on love if it's not working out."

GOD SAYS:
"Get on your knees and pray if it's not working out."

Seek first his kingdom and his righteousness, and all these things will be given to you as well.
MATTHEW 6:33

The old saying goes, "If it gets too hot in the kitchen, get out!" This might apply to kitchens, but it just shouldn't fly when it comes to marriages. Instead, consider the lesson learned from Shadrach, Meshach, and Abednego.

These three Hebrew children refused to bow down to a false God. Instead, they were thrown into a fiery furnace certain to melt even the hardest metals. They knew God could save them, but they also knew heaven would be better than life on a persecuted earth. Once thrown in, not only did they not burn up, but an angel of God appeared and fellow-shipped with them. God showed up at their hottest moment, and they emerged without even a whiff of smoke.

So many people burn up or leave when heat turns up in marriage. These people roll over and become a lifeless shell, dominated or stunned by the sin of their partner. Or they walk out, refusing to even talk with their difficult partner. They also ignore God.

When God is invited into a marriage, He becomes like a third strand of string in a rope. This three-ply rope doesn't break very easily. It holds fast. Even when one partner doesn't want to pray, if the praying partner seeks God in prayer, the marriage has a much better chance of survival. God can grab ahold of the sinning partner and tell him or her to repent.

Other godly practices like giving thanks in all things and serving sacrificially also contribute to preserving marriage. Done in the name of God, while calling on His name, these practices are like curing salts on a ham. They add flavor (fun and joy) and keep it from spoiling (divorce or affairs). Therefore, seek God. He will answer.

Regardless of what else you put on, wear love. It's your basic, all-purpose garment. Never be without it.
Colossians 3:14 msg

THE WORLD SAYS:
"Love is about two people wanting to be together."

GOD SAYS:
"Love is about two people committed to being together through thick and thin."

To the married I command, yet not I but the Lord:
A wife is not to depart from her husband.
1 CORINTHIANS 7:10 NKJV

The young couple loved each other, so they wanted to be together. She made him think. He made her laugh. They spent many carefree days together. But after their wedding, work, obligations, and life crowded out their fun times. Irritating personality quirks blossomed into offensive actions. She spent too much money at the salon. He watched football or played golf instead of doing yard work. They didn't want to be together anymore. They thought about divorce.

Even though they said "till death do us part," the above couple never really committed to each other. In the back of their minds, they always held on to an "escape clause." Hence, they were unprepared for hardship.

A different young couple started out similarly to the one above, but their hardship came in the form of bad health—a stroke. She could hardly talk or feed herself. Her husband prepared meals for her, fed her, bathed her, and clothed her for more than fifty years until she died. He loved his wife and realized that, because of her stroke, he had an opportunity to love her even more deeply—through the treasured fulfillment of the vow of commitment.

If you predetermine to love another despite the circumstances, then you'll be able to endure trials and temptations. You can then hold on and do what it takes to come out on the other side together. Honest communication, planned fun times during busy schedules, prayer, Bible reading, and mutually submitting one to another all become tools to preserve and protect a marriage. Romantic feelings come and go. You might not "feel" like you love her anymore. To make it work, a couple requires mutual, conscientious, consistent effort. After all, love is a choice, not a feeling.

Love never gives up.
1 CORINTHIANS 13:4 MSG

THE WORLD SAYS:
"Love is a fountain of youth."

GOD SAYS:
"Real love is growing old together."

Abraham fell facedown; he laughed and said to himself, "Will a son be born to a man a hundred years old? Will Sarah bear a child at the age of ninety?"

GENESIS 17:17

Some men think wives are like cars. Every so often, they feel the urge to trade in their woman for a younger model. Who doesn't like the lines and curves and color of a fresh off-the-assembly-line roadster? Women aren't cars, however. They have feelings and souls and need to be treasured forever. Everybody faces the ravages of time. Everyone gets wrinkles and gray hair. The outside appearance is bound to change, but inner beauty can grow and develop and be even stronger in old age than in youth.

Some of yesterday's glamour queens preserve their beauty by gracefully transferring it to outward acts expressing their kind hearts. Elizabeth Taylor fought to stop AIDS. The late Audrey Hepburn dedicated her final years to the causes of the world's impoverished children. Other movie stars such as Greta Garbo hid away from society in their later years. Vanity, selfishness, or fear can strike the hearts of those who have the most attractive faces, paralyzing them from doing any public good as they grow older.

Yet the unfading beauty of a gentle and quiet spirit pleases God and man. One of the world's most honored and beautiful women achieved notoriety late in her life. Small, bent, and wrinkled, her smile and acts of service made her a treasure to those she served and an example for those who worked with her. You know her as Mother Teresa.

As a man faithfully sticks with his wife through the years, he can have a front-row seat to her inner beauty. His faithfulness can encourage and nurture her spirit. By mutually supporting and continually loving each other, a couple can find freedom, peace, joy, and beauty to last until their final breath.

Husbands, go all out in love for your wives.

Colossians 3:19 msg

THE WORLD SAYS:
"Love is about me."

GOD SAYS:
"Love is about your mate."

Love cares more for others than for self.
1 Corinthians 13:4 msg

First Corinthians 13 describes love with action verbs that can be applied anywhere, anytime. First Corinthians 13 is all about selflessness and nothing about selfishness. When your spouse can't decide between the blue car or the red car, love is patient. When you're waiting on them to get dressed to go out, there patience applies again. When they come in irritated from a bad day, love is kind. When they get the job promotion and you still languish on the bottom rung, you celebrate their achievement. When they keep messing up, love doesn't shove it in their face. Try applying these action verbs when your spouse doesn't deserve it. Try offering patience and kindness to them when you feel like screaming in their face.

The problem with selfishness is that it's. . .well. . .so selfish. It feeds on itself and then implodes. It demands its own way. Selfish people stop loving and become greedy manipulators. Their only behavior is to coerce someone to do something. A loving marriage cannot survive such treatment for long. Something will have to give. Either the selfishness will have to go or the marriage will. If either partner digs in their heels for a fight to get their own way, love is thrown out the window and you truly become competitors instead of lovers.

Love defuses bombs. It builds bonds. It creates unity and peace. It restores. It's altogether positive and beneficial. None of these wonders can be achieved without selfless love in action. God made us that way, and we would do well to remember it.

Let the peace of Christ keep you in tune with each other, in step with each other. None of this going off and doing your own thing.
COLOSSIANS 3:15 MSG

THE WORLD SAYS:
"Sex is about getting."

GOD SAYS:
"Sex is about giving."

"Give, and it will be given to you. A good measure, pressed down, shaken together and running over, will be poured into your lap. For with the measure you use, it will be measured to you."

LUKE 6:38

Brad told Julie he loved her, but she never really believed him. He never gave her praise or quality time. He always spoke condescendingly to her. She suspected that Brad said these words to her only because she gave him sex. But sex doesn't equal love. Sex is about expressing your mutual love for each other in a marriage relationship, and love always gives.

Though celibate His whole life, Christ's lifestyle offers the best clues on how we should view sex. (Here's a hint: It's not about you.) Christ lived to give. He lived to please others. He sacrificially gave of Himself to enrich humanity. In this same attitude, therefore, the best sex benefits your partner—physically pleasing and emotionally secure.

Think about coercion and stealing. Does it ever really satisfy when you force someone to give you what you want? A thrill might come in the short term, but a caring, understanding recipient would want the giver to be happy. When the giver is thrilled to give the recipient what he or she needs, both giver and recipient are happy. If the giver gives begrudgingly out of duty, anger, fear of punishment, or some other negative reason, joy, strength, and life will soon dry up.

In Ephesians 5, God tells husbands to cherish their wives—the word *cherish* means to emotionally warm or provide security so that the wife doesn't worry about her husband looking over his shoulder at some other woman. When a woman is able to feel secure in her spouse's love, and when a man focuses on meeting her needs, then they will have the most meaningful sexual experience a couple can know.

Don't take advantage of [your spouse].

Colossians 3:19 msg

THE WORLD SAYS:
"Sex is right if you're in love."

GOD SAYS:
"Sex is right if you are married."

*Marriage is honorable among all, and the bed undefiled;
but fornicators and adulterers God will judge.*
HEBREWS 13:4 NKJV

The world often mixes up lust with love. It might say "sex is right if you're in love," when it really means "sex is right if you are in lust." In other words, "If it feels so right, it can't be wrong." Well, it feels right because God made us sexual beings, but it is wrong because marriage is the only appropriate place to express that sexual desire. When sexual desires are acted on outside of marriage, it stems from a craving to gratify one's own needs. God wants sex to enrich each other—to literally seek that person's highest good, which for the unmarried means not to engage in any kind of sexual activity.

Again, God is not anti-sex. He wants us to have great sex. One reason He reserves sex for marriage is so that we might be saved from heartache. Sex bonds people together physically, emotionally, and even spiritually. Breakups rip those bonds apart, causing great pain. Some turn numb to the pain, not able to emotionally connect with any member of the opposite sex.

Others say they need to practice sex before marriage. Nonsense! If you do practice sex with someone other than your marriage partner, you'll always be comparing your spouse with that partner. That's not fair to your spouse and will bring unnecessary and painful thoughts for you, too. You and your marriage partner can enjoy a lifetime of exploring new frontiers of sex together.

Sex is great, but it's not the end-all, be-all expression of love. Some marriages might not even have any sex because of health problems, age, or other issues. But that shouldn't spoil the marriage. Sexually expressive or not, a lasting, loving marriage reflects the beauty of Christ's love for His people.

If we are living in the light of God's presence. . .the blood of Jesus, his Son, cleanses us from every sin.

1 JOHN 1:7 NLT

THE WORLD SAYS:
"Going into marriage, you need experience."

GOD SAYS:
"Going into marriage, you need commitment."

Know therefore that the LORD your God is God; he is the faithful God, keeping his covenant of love to a thousand generations of those who love him and keep his commands.

DEUTERONOMY 7:9

Two prospective employees applied for the same senior management position. Both men had impressive résumés. Michael worked in management for over twenty years in many Fortune 500 companies. He'd show up for work, sometimes saw improvements, and then found a reason to leave. He had lots of experience but never stayed around long enough to enjoy long-term company growth. Matthew, however, had lesser management experience. He was younger and had worked with only one other company before. Even so, he worked there for ten years, saw phenomenal growth, and still considered his former employer a treasured friend and mentor. Who do you think eventually got the job? Michael or Matthew?

Employers (and conscientious, godly spouse candidates) want someone who isn't afraid of commitment. They want a team player who will stick with the program through thick and thin.

People who go from job to job (and from bed to bed) practice and condition themselves only to cut and run. Sure, they get experience, but they don't have what it takes to make a lasting, winning combination.

God designed marriage to be a reflection of His love for humanity. His love toward His human creation never fails—ever! He's looking for a bride that will be a team player and will stick with the program. He wants to celebrate with you on the last day. He wants to lift you into the air, smile wide, and pop the sparkling cider. Therefore, love your spouse wholeheartedly with a long-term goal of sticking it through to the end. If you are "experienced," it's not too late to turn into a committed team player. Seek restoration from God, and learn the depths of His commitment to you!

[Love] never looks back.
1 CORINTHIANS 13:7 MSG

THE WORLD SAYS:
"Keep nagging until you get what you want."

GOD SAYS:
"A quarrelsome wife is like a constant dripping on a rainy day."

It is better to live alone in the corner of an attic than with a contentious wife in a lovely home.
PROVERBS 21:9 NLT

Sam felt like World War III had just hit his house. His wife got on his case for every little thing, and now she was screaming. He couldn't understand why putting the toilet seat down was so important. He thought he was a good husband. And in many ways he was. But what he wasn't good at was listening. He didn't show the kind of love she really wanted and needed for peace and security. The toilet seat problem was only the expression of a deeper issue—their inability to mutually submit one to another in love.

Choose your battles. If every minor issue in marriage becomes a major issue, then your life will be filled with constant strife. So what if the dishes don't get done right away? Better a dirty house with love than a clean house with animosity and resentment. Marriage is work. But when you choose your battles and take issue only when it is absolutely necessary, you can spend more time loving each other. And by loving and serving each other, you can cover over the multitude of little things that in the big picture really aren't consequential. Plus, when your spouse feels valued and appreciated by your attention, he or she might be more likely to remember the little thing that concerns you. A happy husband pleased with his wife just might remember to put down the toilet seat after using it.

Nagging might achieve some short-term results. It might cause your spouse to change out of anger or fear that you'll continue your negativity. But lasting change comes by gentle instruction, love, and mercy, and a mind committed to loving another. Husbands and wives leave the wars to the battlefields and keep them out of their homes.

[Love] doesn't fly off the handle.
1 CORINTHIANS 13:5 MSG

THE WORLD SAYS:
"It's funny to call my wife 'the old ball and chain.'"

GOD SAYS:
"He who finds a wife finds a good thing and obtains favor from the Lord."

He who finds a wife finds what is good and receives favor from the LORD.
PROVERBS 18:22

Frank thought it was funny when he sang, "The old gray mare—she ain't what she used to be" to his wife on her fiftieth birthday. Everyone laughed, including his wife, Marie, but inside she felt devalued. His gag gift, a box of adult diapers, underscored her pain.

She wouldn't mind the joking if she felt loved and accepted by her husband. But he spent more time with his hunting and fishing buddies than he did with her. Their interaction was civil but not very loving or compassionate. She wondered if Frank would be more attentive to a younger, more attractive wife. She doubted if Frank would ever really miss her if she were gone. She felt like an impediment to his happiness instead of an asset. She felt like "the old ball and chain."

The Bible says, "Words carry the power to bless or to curse" (see James 3:10 NRSV). Frank called Marie "an old ball and chain," but he didn't anticipate the consequences. He didn't realize an old ball and chain can't warm up. It can't love back. And it's meant to enslave the wearer.

The reason Frank went off so much is that he did think of Marie as an impediment. In reality, his words and actions impeded her. She couldn't offer life and freedom because she needed to feel love in order to give it. If Frank had spoken encouraging words to her, and then backed that up with loving actions, she would have gladly reciprocated the favor. Instead, she dutifully cooked, cleaned, and performed her wifely obligations without enthusiasm. If Frank recognized these "blessings" and honored her for them, he would find reason enough to stick around the house more. He'd find more than an impediment. He'd find a valued partner in adventure, love, and life.

Out of respect for Christ, be courteously reverent to one another.
EPHESIANS 5:21 MSG

THE WORLD SAYS:
"A little sex never hurt anyone."

GOD SAYS:
"Flee immorality."

[Potiphar's wife] caught [Joseph] by his cloak and said, "Come to bed with me!" But he left his cloak in her hand and ran out of the house.

GENESIS 39:12

Alan's coworkers thought he didn't like women. He never watched pornography. He never made lascivious comments toward women. He wouldn't join them to go nightclubbing. Alan wouldn't even make romantic advances toward any of the attractive girls they tried to set him up with. When his coworkers hired a prostitute to foist herself on him, he ran off without touching her. He wasn't gay. He simply was looking forward to great sex—with his future wife.

Alan had other reasons, too, for celibacy. He didn't want the emotional baggage that sex brings into a relationship. He didn't want to be a "former" lover to a woman who had to explain her sexual history to her new husband. Mostly, he just didn't want to displease God.

Joseph of the Old Testament ran when Potiphar's wife tried to seduce him. He said, "How can I do such an evil thing to my Lord?" (see Genesis 39:9). He didn't want to hurt God or Potiphar either. He respected both too much to hurt them. He also respected himself.

God doesn't want to spoil your fun. He created sex and knows how fun it can be. He's not asking you to flee sex (though He might call some to lifelong celibacy). He's only asking you to flee inappropriate sex. And sex with anyone other than your heterosexual marriage partner is inappropriate and immoral.

It's a lie that "a little sex never hurt anyone." It hurts both partners, and it hurts God. There might not seem to be any immediate pain or cost to sex outside of marriage, but God calls it a sin. Instead, wait until marriage, remain faithful in it, and discover just how great sex God's way can be.

What happens when we live God's way? He brings gifts into our lives. . . . We develop. . .a conviction that a basic holiness permeates things and people.
GALATIANS 5:22 MSG

THE WORLD SAYS:
"I can look as long as I don't touch."

GOD SAYS:
"The eyes are the window to your heart."

I tell you that anyone who looks at a woman lustfully has already committed adultery with her in his heart.

MATTHEW 5:28

Jim thought he had found the perfect solution. He knew scripture forbade premarital sex, but like any red-blooded young man, he had a strong sex drive. Hence, he decided to keep it all in his mind. He'd sexually fantasize about attractive women he'd meet and befriend. Occasionally he would fantasize while looking at pornography, too. He fed his active imagination with dream girls who never required anything of him but who always gave of themselves willingly. Jim had an active sex life in his mind. What he didn't have was healthy relationships with members of the opposite sex on any realistic level.

God calls sexual fantasizing sin. Imaginary sex also creates an artificial, emotional bond with your mental partner, and they don't even know it. While they may see you as a casual friend, you see them as a sort of surrogate spouse. Hence, you relate to each other on two completely different levels. Intellectually, you can admit you aren't married to your imaginary spouse, but your feelings don't always correspond to this. Let's say this other person wants to casually date other people. Because you have bonded with him or her in your mind, you may get jealous over their normal behavior. This person might enjoy light conversation with you, but you get too personal with them, assuming you have a level of intimacy that doesn't exist.

The sexual urge is strong. God made us that way. If you learn to control your thoughts and accept God's grace to help you overcome temptations, you'll please Him, gain self-respect, learn to relate to people of the opposite sex in a natural and healthy way, and in so doing, position yourself for a long-term marriage relationship including good sex. Again, God's way proves to be the better plan.

Treat the older women as you would your mother, and treat the younger women with all purity as your own sisters.

1 TIMOTHY 5:2 NLT

THE WORLD SAYS:
"It's a shame to be a virgin."

GOD SAYS:
"It's an honor to be a virgin."

God blesses those whose hearts are pure, for they will see God.
MATTHEW 5:8 NLT

One of the breakout movie hits of 2005 was *The 40-Year-Old Virgin*. Disguised as a run-of-the-mill sex comedy, its final message suggests righteousness. The hero, awkward Andy Stizer (played by Steve Carell), is a forty-year-old who hasn't had sex yet. When he meets Trish, he meets the love of his life. Though they attempt sex, they ultimately realize it's best to wait until marriage. As Andy's coworkers watch this love affair blossom, they admit that their sexual past has only brought them heartache and pain.

Virginity brings great benefits. Virgins don't have sexually transmitted diseases. They don't have to worry about the consequences of unplanned or unwanted pregnancies. They don't have to sexually compare their future spouse to any other person. They don't have the pain of bonding with another only to see that bond ripped apart by someone moving on to the next partner. They have never had their sexual desires "awakened," therefore, they can't miss it or crave it. They have minds and emotions free to think on the things of God.

The world tries to shame virgins and make fun of them. But teens and singles everywhere are making their voice heard. Purity rings sell steadily. The "Why Wait?" program rolls on. Various best-selling Christian musicians and artists proudly declare their virginity. They want young people to know: "It's cool to be a virgin."

If you have already had sex, God can still heal and seal your heart. Ask Him to renew a right spirit within you. Your soul can be pure once again. In today's sex-saturated society, temptations to have sex abound, but if you preserve sex until marriage, you'll please God and give yourself and your partner a great gift.

Let's make a clean break with everything that defiles or distracts us, both within and without. Let's make our entire lives fit and holy temples for the worship of God.

2 CORINTHIANS 7:1 MSG

THE WORLD SAYS:
"When dating, just don't go all the way."

GOD SAYS:
"When dating, treat your date with the respect you would show your sister or brother."

How delightful is your love, my sister, my bride!
SONG OF SOLOMON 4:10

Youth counselors all recognize the number-one question teens have when it comes to sex: "How far can I go?" Wise youth counselors know that this isn't even the right question. What Christianity demands—or better stated, what God demands—isn't a gradient scale of acceptable or unacceptable sexual behavior. What God demands is faithfulness to Him and obedience to His ways.

For some dating couples, even a goodnight kiss might be too far. Such a couple might arouse desires by that kiss that would lead to inappropriate sexual activity. Such couples might want to wait until their wedding night to give a kiss, because only then their desire for one another could be consummated in a holy manner.

The body of Christ is a family. We are all brothers and sisters. (Even nonbelievers should be treated like family members who haven't been adopted yet.) No brother or sister rightfully engages in sexual activity with one another. Instead, they play, talk, eat, and help each other. They encourage each other to develop into greater representatives of Christ.

Any physical activity performed to satisfy lust or that leads to greater temptation should be avoided. Many Christian leaders agree that holding hands and light kissing is as far as any unmarried couple should go. Through resisting temptation and keeping oneself pure, couples can actually create more desire for each other, which can later be satisfied within marriage. Good-bye gestures like a hug or a light kiss might not be as fun in the short term as sex, but until you make that long-term commitment in the bond of marriage, anything more results in sin and hardship for everyone involved. Instead of looking at what you are missing, recognize the benefits, pleasures, and relief of a heart and life of purity and right standing before God.

Let every detail in your lives—words, actions, whatever—be done in the name of the Master, Jesus.
COLOSSIANS 3:17 MSG

THE WORLD SAYS:
"It's just natural for teens to be crazy for the opposite sex."

GOD SAYS:
"You are more than a body; you're a person created in My image."

God created man in his own image, in the image of God he created him; male and female he created them.

GENESIS 1:27

Sixteen-year-old Carter felt like an animal whenever pretty teen girls in tight clothes walked by. Sex weighed heavily on his mind. Carter thought, *God made me male. He made me with hormones. He made me a sexual being. Why shouldn't I act on those sexual urges?* One day a particularly stunning young girl walked in front of him. He couldn't help noticing her. Then she turned around. There in front of him in a short miniskirt and blue eye shadow stood Ashley, his twin sister! Carter felt disgusted with himself. And embarrassed for Ashley. It made him sad to see that she was turning into someone much like himself.

Carter knew Ashley had a heart for God. He couldn't understand why she was trying to vamp it up. He knew she was so much more than a piece of flesh. He knew God lived within her. She had giving hands, lips quick to sing God's praise, and a sharp mind dedicated to study. She knew better, but, like Carter, her hormones and peer pressure were getting the best of her.

When Carter realized that women were more than flesh and blood, but were people created in God's image, he never quite looked at them in the same way. Sure, their form still excited him, but he knew they had stuff between their ears and in their hearts, too. God did a work in Carter's heart and mind to temper the hormones raging in his body. May He do the same with you as you live and serve together as brothers and sisters in Christ.

Keep my decrees and laws,
for the man who obeys them will live by them.
LEVITICUS 18:5

THE WORLD SAYS:
"Use protection."

GOD SAYS
"Use self-control."

The fruit of the Spirit is love, joy, peace, patience, kindness, goodness, faithfulness, gentleness and self-control. Against such things there is no law.

GALATIANS 5:22–23

The movement has grown across America. Teenagers are pledging to wait until marriage to have sex. What? It can't be! Everyone knows teenagers can't help themselves. All teenagers are having sex, so in order to stop teen pregnancy and STDs, we give them protection. Right? Wrong! There is no condom that can protect and wrap a human heart.

Abstinence-only messages resonate with young people. Discerning young people are beginning to learn that the price is too high to pay for premarital sexual activity. When you leave sex out of the equation, you get to know members of the opposite sex for who they really are. You get to know their minds, hearts, likes, dislikes, and sense of humor. Sex muddles all this and makes it more difficult to see the real person. Premarital sex offers "sex-goggles" to the practitioner—making them see what they want to see in their partner instead of what is really there. Self-control must be implemented to see the truth.

Self-control has a lot to do with "sublimation." It means "the redirection of instinctual drives for long-term goals." By delaying sexual gratification and release, God is not trying to limit our joy—but to increase it. He doesn't want us to have bad memories of other sexual experiences.

It's time that we grow up and listen to the One who created sex in the first place. God is not anti-sex—He told Adam and Eve to have sex, to reproduce. . .and that was before they had eaten of the forbidden fruit. Sex can wait. It has to—for the good of you and your spouse. It'll be waiting there, ready for you to enjoy at the proper time.

Love doesn't want what it doesn't have.
1 Corinthians 13:4 msg

THE WORLD SAYS:
"Beauty is skin deep."

GOD SAYS:
"Beauty is an inside job."

Charm is deceptive, and beauty is fleeting;
but a woman who fears the LORD is to be praised.
PROVERBS 31:30

In her youth, Anastasia was considered a world-class beauty. Perfect skin, long legs, button nose, and a thin figure, she frequently won beauty contests and even entered the Ms. World competition. Her beauty brought her fame and fortune. Life couldn't have been better for Anastasia—until she turned forty. At forty, her skin began to wrinkle and sag. Fewer offers came in. At forty-two, her hair started to turn gray. By forty-five, nobody wanted her face and body anymore. Anastasia had become a has-been. Unaccustomed to such treatment, Anastasia did all she could to hold on to her youth. Facial treatments turned into face-lifts. Leg lifts turned into liposuction. Reconstructive surgery became as often and as normal for her as dental visits. Anastasia placed her worth on her outward beauty, and in return, her outside looked fake and her inside turned dry and ugly.

Sadly, Anastasia never learned how to nurture her inner beauty. For decades, she rode on the praises of others who commented on her outward appearance. She never considered what time would do to her body as she got older. Yet it wasn't hard to forgive Anastasia for her vanity. Growing up, her parents never valued her or praised her inner qualities. They didn't give her much at all except the bare necessities for survival. They were too consumed in their own vanity projects.

No matter your age, encourage inner beauty with one another. Treasure and praise your mothers and grandmothers for their service and gentle, giving spirits. Teach younger women to value character and personality. Let them know that they are loved and cherished no matter if they are tall, short, thick, or thin. A kind, gentle, giving, loving woman is beautiful no matter her age or body size.

Chosen by God for this new life of love,
dress in the wardrobe God picked out for you: compassion,
kindness, humility, quiet strength, discipline.
COLOSSIANS 3:12 MSG

THE WORLD SAYS:
"Who cares if I break my marriage vows?"

GOD SAYS:
"I care."

[Be] trustworthy in everything.
1 TIMOTHY 3:11

Have you ever told a trusted friend you would help them out, but you decided to do something else instead? How did you both feel when they found out about it? Cheating on your spouse is no different than letting a friend down. In fact, it's worse because you made a commitment to your spouse before God in front of witnesses. But why does God care? What difference does it make?

God cares because He wants your best. Your spouse was given to you to enjoy forever. Your spouse offers you stability and security. Your physical relationship with your spouse is sacred, reflecting Christ's intense love for His bride, the Church. When you violate that sacred trust, you stop representing Christ and His love for His people. You tell others, "My word doesn't matter. I especially don't care about how I represent Christ." Actions speak louder than words. How you treat others, especially in your closest relationships, speaks volumes about your relationship with God.

Perhaps you feel God has let you down in your marriage and so you have to take matters into your own hands. Maybe you feel like your spouse isn't holding up his or her end of the bargain so you feel license to roam. Your marital pain might be God's way of trying to get your attention. Perhaps He wants to give you something better. Not another spouse or even another lover, but maybe He wants you to learn from Him how to treat your spouse differently. Maybe He wants to correct your attitude.

Marriage is tough work. There's no getting around it. But the rewards of sticking to your vows and doing the hard work to maintain and improve your marriage offers rewards that no mere fling could ever achieve.

Guard the spirit of marriage within you.
Don't cheat on your spouse.
MALACHI 2:15 MSG

THE WORLD SAYS:
"It's ridiculous to think we'll still love each other in thirty years."

GOD SAYS:
"Love isn't a dream; it's a choice."

Give thanks to the LORD, for he is good; his love endures forever.
1 CHRONICLES 16:34

After most people retire and spend the rest of their lives in leisure, Barb and Rick decided to start a new ministry on their fortieth wedding anniversary. They decided to mentor and instruct young couples on maintaining a thriving, strong marriage. They saw the incredible need to promote long-lasting marriage and decided to do something about it.

What is more difficult to imagine? That you'll fall out of love in thirty years or that you'll still be in love in thirty years? Who put this idea into your head that love lasts only for a short while? Hollywood and the world at large report on disposable romances that are discarded at the first sign of trouble. But do these publicized relationships represent the real world? Do they represent God's way?

God wants you to stay together until "death do you part." He has a lifetime of love that He wants to live through you and your spouse. His love has no time limit or expiration dates.

It's getting harder and harder to see good examples of lasting marriages. Many of today's young, marrying-age people are children of divorce. They haven't seen their parents grow old together. If this describes you, seek out and befriend older couples who have been married for a long time. Observe them and ask them what the secret to their long marriage is. Ask them if they have been tempted to discard their marriage, and then ask them what they did to preserve it.

Love can be maintained for thirty-plus years. Many in our oldest generation still understand the value of commitment and sticking to one's word. You'll never discover the blessing of a long marriage and lasting love until you make a commitment to partake in that adventure yourself.

Instruct and direct one another using good common sense.
And sing, sing your hearts out to God!
Colossians 3:16 msg

THE WORLD SAYS:
"Sex is everything."

GOD SAYS:
"Sex is a part of a healthy marriage."

Do not deprive each other except by mutual consent and for a time, so that you may devote yourselves to prayer. Then come together again so that Satan will not tempt you because of your lack of self-control.

1 CORINTHIANS 7:5

Tony and Gwen loved sex. They often made love several times a day. It was their favorite activity and reason for living. They thought constant sex would keep their marriage exciting. Soon, however, it became lifeless and laborious. Instead of a fun, mutual expression of love for each other, it became a chore. To make it exciting and fresh, it also got perverted. Tony and Gwen began to disrespect each other and God. They tried to make sex everything, and in the process it became nothing.

Imagine a Thanksgiving dinner. On the tables rests turkey, dressing, potatoes, gravy, and more. But suppose you were especially looking forward to eating dessert: hot apple pie with ice cream on top. You've been thinking about that apple pie so much you can smell it in your mind. That Thanksgiving Day, you can't even see the other food. You eat one piece of pie, then another, and another. It's great, but now you start to look at the other foods. Then you look at that pie again, and think, *I need to eat another piece.* So you do, and then you get sick. Nothing else at the table looks good to eat at all.

This is what a marriage that focuses only on sex looks like. If you focus only on sex, you'll miss out on all the other goodies, and you'll get sick. A marriage built only on sex unravels. A healthy marriage with sex as a part of it is like a fantastic meal, filled with all sorts of treats and delights. Plus, it's good for you!

A person without self-control is as defenseless as a city with broken-down walls.
Proverbs 25:28 NLT

THE WORLD SAYS:
"Pornography doesn't hurt anyone."

GOD SAYS:
"Pornography hurts everyone it touches—especially you."

The prostitute reduces you to a loaf of bread,
and the adulteress preys upon your very life.
PROVERBS 6:26

In his book *Mere Christianity,* writer C. S. Lewis asks his reader to "imagine a country where you could fill a theater by simply bringing a covered plate onto the stage and then slowly lifting the cover" to reveal the food. He adds, "Would you not think that in that country, something had gone wrong with the appetite for food?" Lewis then compares that abnormality to the sexual appetite fulfilled though peep shows and pornography. It's equally strange and equally wrong.

Pornography hurts everyone involved. The porn actor loses self-respect and dignity through undressing and performing sex acts on camera. Many of these actors have to disassociate their minds from their real selves. Some even have a "no kissing" rule, reserving this special act for those they truly love. This suggests that they are trying to hold on to something pure while giving their bodies away.

Porn hurts marriages because it says the husband/wife bond isn't really sacred. Porn disrespects the vows of marriage. It's like introducing a stranger into the bedroom. Pornography, therefore, means unfaithfulness in every sense of the word.

Pornography hurts children, too. Daddies (and Mommies) who use pornography set a poor example for their kids and expose them to sights and visuals they should never see. They also communicate that sex isn't special but just a plaything or a toy.

Finally, pornography hurts the viewer. It's bait and fuel for sexual addiction. It offers an easy but still sinful way to be unfaithful to their spouses and loved ones. It cheapens relationships with the opposite sex. It objectifies and devalues women (and men). God has such a garden of delights for married couples. Why spoil it by introducing to it a stranger who takes and never gives?

Turn my eyes from worthless things.
PSALM 119:37 NLT

THE WORLD SAYS:
"You always hurt the one you love."

GOD SAYS:
"Be tenderhearted and kind toward one another."

A kindhearted [person] gains respect.
PROVERBS 11:16

You and another shopper both reach for the last pint of strawberries. You graciously step back and urge her to take them, while she smiles and does the same to you. After many assurances she finally takes them, thanking you profusely. You finish your errands and head home. You put the groceries on the counter and flop down on the couch to watch TV. Your spouse is vacuuming, the phone is ringing, and someone is at the door. You turn the volume up so you can hear your show.

Why do we tend to be more kind, polite, and gracious to strangers than we are to those we love the most? If we are honest with ourselves, we would have to admit that being polite to a stranger doesn't take much effort, but showing true kindness to the people we live with every day, year after year. . .that takes some work.

What might happen if you were as polite and gracious to your spouse, your children, or your closest friends as you are to the people you meet as you go about your day? What if you opened the door for your spouse just like you do for the elderly lady who is following you into the store? What if you dropped what you were doing to help a friend with a problem, just as you would stop to help a stranger pick up a dropped package?

Yes, kindness takes effort. It is easy to forget to make that effort with those you love—to take them for granted. Even if you aren't being deliberately unkind, you can still hurt your loved ones when you are careless about showing them love. But when you work at being truly kind and tenderhearted, your relationships will grow and thrive. As the old saying goes, "Those who plant kindness will reap a harvest of love."

Let us not become weary in doing good, for at the proper time we will reap a harvest if we do not give up.

GALATIANS 6:9

THE WORLD SAYS:
"We don't need God. We have each other."

GOD SAYS:
"My love makes your love possible."

We love because he first loved us.
1 JOHN 4:19

A flower can be planted in the most fertile soil and be watered with abundant rains, but if it is kept in the darkness, away from the sun, it will wither and die. You can buy the most advanced, state-of-the-art computer with super-fast processing and a massive amount of memory. But if you don't plug it in, that computer is nothing more than a very expensive plastic box. You can give a child all the toys that he could ever want, but if you don't feed him, what good will even the most lavish gifts do him?

You may be thinking, *Well, of course. It's just common sense that flowers need sunlight, computers need electricity, and children need food!* Just as elementary as these concepts is the fact that to sustain true love, you must receive it from the Source—God. The Bible says that not only is God loving, He *is* love (see 1 John 4:16). So, just as impossible as it is for a flower to live off of soil and water alone, or for a computer to "will" itself to work without electricity, or for a child to survive without food, it is also impossible for love to last without God.

Relationships built on the foundation of human love alone quickly crumble under the weight of difficulties. Human love is imperfect and limited. But relationships that draw their power from the eternal Source of love—from God Himself—can withstand even the toughest times. God's love is everlasting, perfect, and limitless.

So like a flower, turn your faces toward the warmth of God's love. Plug your hearts into His power. Open your hands, and trust Him to feed your soul like a loving Father. When you do, your love will grow in beauty, power, and strength—God will help you build a love that lasts a lifetime.

We know and rely on the love God has for us. God is love. Whoever lives in love lives in God, and God in him.

1 JOHN 4:16

THE WORLD SAYS:
"Maybe a child can save our marriage."

GOD SAYS:
"Only I can save your marriage."

My soul finds rest in God alone; my salvation comes from him.
PSALM 62:1

Looking into the face of a newborn baby is an amazing experience, especially when that baby is your own. The world is a new and wonderful place when you see it through the eyes of a child. Children are truly a gift from God. They bring hope and joy and inspire a deep love that knows no equal.

While children are wonderful blessings, some people place an unfair burden upon these little ones. A young marriage gets rocky, and instead of doing the hard work of learning to love each other God's way, the couple decides that a baby will be the glue that will hold them together. What an impossible task for a tiny child!

Sadly, couples soon realize that having a child is more than sweet little coos and adorable smiles. With babies come huge responsibilities, sleepless nights, and more than a few moments of frustration. Without a solid foundation of a stable marriage, the inherent struggles of parenthood can cause a relationship to fall apart.

A little child can never be your salvation—only God can bring healing and restoration to your marriage. God wants to be a partner in your relationship. He wants to bless you with the strength, perseverance, and love that you need to go the distance with your spouse. When you turn your problems over to Him, you are turning to the true Source of help. God promises to mend your broken hearts and to bring you hope and understanding in the midst of your hurt.

So when you find yourself struggling in your relationship, go to the Creator of marriage. Let Him do the work in your heart that only He can do. Then, when your marriage is strong in the power of the Lord, you'll be ready to receive the wonderful blessing of a precious child.

Children are a gift from the LORD; they are a reward from him.
PSALM 127:3 NLT

THE WORLD SAYS:
"Love conquers all."

GOD SAYS:
"My love conquers all."

Love never gives up.
1 CORINTHIANS 13:7 NLT

The beautiful maiden sits alone in a cold, stone room in a high, dark tower. Far below a fearsome dragon guards the gate. Suddenly the dragon screams, and from her small window the maiden sees a gallant knight bravely fighting the beast. The battle is fierce, but the knight prevails. He climbs the tower and frees the princess, and together they ride to his castle where she becomes his cherished bride. Love has conquered all, and they live happily ever after.

You've heard this story a million times, and yet it still tugs at your heart. Perhaps this story resonates with us all because it is the story we all long to live. We all want to believe that love will conquer all our pain. We long to be so loved that we are worth fighting for or to have someone in our lives who will inspire us to be brave and gallant. And yet, in the real world, love often seems too fragile to conquer the hurts in our relationships, and we're left wondering if anything can heal our broken hearts.

The wonderful news is that love does indeed conquer all. Love Himself came to our rescue in the form of a humble Jewish man named Jesus. He came into the darkness of our world and its pain and fought the ultimate battle with the "dragons" of sin and death. He gave up His own life for us and then rose from the dead so that death could never touch us. And now, through Jesus, we can live in the power of true love—God's strong, eternal love that does indeed conquer all. When you call out for rescue, the Prince of Peace will come to your aid. Your most troubled relationships will be healed, your broken heart will be mended, and Love will truly conquer all!

Love will last forever.
1 CORINTHIANS 13:8 NLT

THE WORLD SAYS:
"I love him—even though he doesn't share my faith."

GOD SAYS:
"Don't join yourself to an unbeliever."

Do not be mismatched with unbelievers.
2 CORINTHIANS 6:14 NRSV

Tolerance and open-mindedness—these seem to be the highest values of our society. Respecting the beliefs of others is good and healthy. You can grow and become more compassionate when you honor others and their opinions. But when it comes to committing yourself to another, you must be very careful about giving your heart to someone who doesn't share your faith in God.

Avoiding romantic relationships with people who don't share your beliefs may seem old-fashioned or even prejudicial. But God discourages this for a reason—He wants to protect your heart. God says that to marry an unbeliever will keep you from growing and reaching your goals. You'll be torn between your love for your spouse and your love for God. There are many examples in the Bible of the disastrous results of falling in love with someone who doesn't share your faith. One of the most extreme is the story of a man named Samson, who ended up imprisoned and blinded when the woman he loved betrayed him to his enemies!

The Bible says that marriage between a Christian and an unbeliever is like harnessing two oxen together that are unequal in their strength and purpose. As a result, they pull in opposite directions, getting nowhere. If you and your spouse are constantly pulling in the opposite directions, your marriage will bring you both nothing but frustration and heartache.

When a husband and wife share the same faith, they can work together toward the same goals. They grow together. Their loyalty won't be divided because they share a love for their heavenly Father.

When you seek to follow God's Word and avoid romantic relationships with those who don't share your faith, God will be faithful to provide you with the love that you long for—a love that will bring you true joy and fulfillment.

> *"I know the plans I have for you,"* declares the LORD,
> *"plans to prosper you and not to harm you, plans to give you
> hope and a future."*
> JEREMIAH 29:11

THE WORLD SAYS:
*"Our marriage is strong;
we don't need anyone else."*

GOD SAYS:
*"Strong marriages are
God-centered marriages."*

A cord of three strands is not quickly broken.
ECCLESIASTES 4:12

You are hanging, suspended in midair, as you climb the sheer rock face of a huge and imposing cliff. All that stands between you and falling to the forest floor far below is a single rope. All your hopes rest on the strength of that rope. If it holds firm, you'll reach the summit and enjoy a breathtaking view. If it breaks under the stress of the climb, all hope is lost. With so much at stake, would you rather that your rope be made of two cords or three? Obviously, a rope made of three cords woven into one will be stronger and better able to support you during the long climb.

When your marriage is new and fresh, it is easy to think that you have all you need in each other. You're in love, you're together, and your future is ahead of you. What more could you possibly ask for? But then, things get tough. You have financial struggles. Children come along and bring with them the challenges of parenthood. Life gets busy and stressful. You look around and find that your marriage is starting to look a little frayed around the edges. You wonder if it will hold up under the strain.

God wants to be the third cord in your marriage—intimately intertwined into your relationship. With His strength and power, you and your spouse can face even the toughest challenges. You can be confident that your marriage is strong enough to stand the test.

So how do you bring God into your relationship? Open your hearts to His love and guidance. Read the Bible together and encourage each other to put God's Word into practice. Pray together, and pray for each other. As you seek God together, He will become a Partner in your marriage, strengthen your bond, and help you create a love that lasts a lifetime.

The Lord is the strength of his people.
Psalm 28:8

THE WORLD SAYS:
"Women manipulate men; it's all part of the game."

GOD SAYS:
"A deceitful tongue crushes the spirit."

An honest answer is like a kiss on the lips.
PROVERBS 24:26

Little white lies—they are one of the main ingredients in every romantic comedy ever to grace the silver screen. Everything is going great for our hero and heroine until he discovers that she wasn't who she said she was, or that she really has a boyfriend, or that she only started dating him to win a bet, but now she really does love him. And then, of course, comes the big confrontation, the crying, and the apologies. The hero, hurt and confused, drives away, or heads to the airport to fly out of her life, or quickly gets engaged to another woman whom he doesn't really love. But always, in the end, after a frantic chase or an interrupted wedding, the couple is reunited and all is forgiven.

This scenario rarely plays out the same way in the real world, and yet women still lie and manipulate men as if they are Julia Roberts in the latest big-screen blockbuster. They play games—hoping to win a man's heart with the help of some little white lies—figuring all will be forgiven when he falls in love with them. Most men, though, are not impressed by manipulation. When he discovers that you've been dishonest, his trust in you, the foundation of any lasting relationship, is broken. And trust is not easily or quickly mended.

For true and lasting love, men need and want to be treated with respect and care, which means avoiding the mind games and manipulation. Being honest and open can be scary, but when you take the risk to truly be yourself, you'll begin building a solid foundation for a strong and lasting relationship. Honesty may not be the best policy when it comes to writing a hit romantic comedy, but it is certainly a vital ingredient to a successful, real-life romance.

You desire honesty from the heart, [Lord.]
PSALM 51:6 NLT

THE WORLD SAYS:
"Men are superior to women."

GOD SAYS:
"There is no male or female in My kingdom."

There is neither. . .male nor female,
for you are all one in Christ Jesus.
GALATIANS 3:28

In spite of the feminist movement and the push for equal rights for women over the past few decades, some men still see themselves as somehow better than women. This prejudice still shows up in many ways in our society today. Many women get lower salaries than their male colleagues receive for doing the same work. Women who choose the high calling of motherhood over a career are often referred to as "just housewives." Many men still regard women as weak, too emotional, or as "just a pretty face."

Women are understandably upset and hurt by these notions. But some wrongly believe that the Bible perpetuates these ideas. God's opinion of women is actually one of high value and true equality. The Bible says that we are all created in God's image and that we are equal in His sight. He doesn't see us as male or female, but as His beloved children—all loved equally and deeply. We, in turn, should treat each other with the respect we all deserve as image-bearers of our Creator. We are to treat each other with gentleness and compassion. And we are to value the special gifts and abilities that we have each been given.

Women have so many unique qualities that are desperately needed in our world today. When men encourage women to use their gifts and to pursue their passions, not only will they please God, they will also discover what amazing talents women have.

Far from diminishing his masculinity, a man who makes the effort to show women that they are highly valued and respected is fulfilling one of his God-given purposes. And a woman who seeks to live out the call that God has given her gives the world a special and unique gift that could come only from her heart.

Be imitators of God, therefore, as dearly loved children and live a life of love.
EPHESIANS 5:1–2

THE WORLD SAYS:
"Why tie yourself down to one person?"

GOD SAYS:
"Without commitment, love cannot grow."

Place me like a seal over your heart, like a seal on your arm.
SONG OF SONGS 8:6

Would you ride a roller coaster without a safety harness? The ride might start out as fun, but it would quickly become very frightening. You wouldn't enjoy the thrill because you'd be too preoccupied with the fear of getting hurt. Instead of feeling the wind in your hair and checking out the awesome view from the top, you'd have your eyes closed tight and a white-knuckled grip on your seat.

Most people would never think of whipping around on a roller coaster without some kind of restraint. But when you have intimate relationships, especially physically intimate relationships without any commitment, you are putting yourself in danger. You're also missing out on the exhilaration and joy that God wants you to experience.

Yes, it is true that "playing the field" and "messing around" can be pretty thrilling in the beginning. But sooner or later you find yourself spinning out of control, struggling to keep your heart from getting hurt. Fear and doubt set in, and instead of enjoying your relationship, you find yourself resorting to suspicion and manipulation. The ride is no longer fun.

But when you seek and find a true and pure commitment, specifically the commitment of marriage, you'll find the security you need to grow true love. Commitment is like that seatbelt on the roller coaster. When you feel safe, assured that you won't fall, you are free to enjoy the ride without fear. You can raise your arms and shout with joy, reveling in the exhilaration.

Far from "tying you down," commitment actually brings great freedom. When you know that your relationship is solid, you can be yourself. You don't have to hold on for dear life, fearing that your loved one will slip away if you relax. Commitment is God's plan for bringing you a truly fulfilling relationship. He wants you to enjoy the ride!

I am my lover's, and my lover is mine. He grazes among the lilies!
Song of Songs 6:3 NLT

THE WORLD SAYS:
"The most important thing is physical attraction."

GOD SAYS:
"Charm is deceptive, and beauty is fleeting."

Don't be concerned about the outward beauty that depends on fancy hairstyles, expensive jewelry, or beautiful clothes. You should be known for the beauty that comes from within, the unfading beauty of a gentle and quiet spirit, which is so precious to God.

1 PETER 3:3–4 NLT

A recent survey of teenage girls revealed that the most requested "Sweet Sixteen" birthday gift is not a car or jewelry, but breast implants! While this fact may seem shocking at first glance, we really shouldn't be surprised. Everywhere you look, the world is telling you that physical beauty is the key to finding happiness. Fashion magazines show men with perfectly chiseled bodies and women showcasing their beauty in alluring poses. You can find some kind of makeover show on TV every night of the week. *Do whatever it takes to achieve society's standard of physical perfection, and the rest of your life will fall into place. Your great looks will attract the man or woman of your dreams, and you'll live happily ever after.* At least that's the message the world is broadcasting.

The truth is, though, that physical beauty is the least important ingredient of a truly fulfilling relationship. You can see the evidence of this fact in Hollywood relationships. Two of the most beautiful celebrities marry, and before they even reach their first anniversary they are signing divorce papers. In spite of the incredibly strong physical attraction that brought them together, their relationship ends up empty and broken. God's warning proves true: "Charm is deceptive, and beauty is fleeting" (Proverbs 31:30). Outer beauty fails to bring inner joy.

So what is the secret of finding that one true love and building a lasting relationship? God's Word tells us that when we cultivate inner beauty by seeking Him, everything else truly will fall into place. When you allow God to do a "makeover" on your heart, the light of His love will shine through you. The radiance of a life transformed by God's love is incredibly attractive—it's a beauty that will not fade with age and never goes out of style.

[God] has made everything beautiful in its time.
ECCLESIASTES 3:11

THE WORLD SAYS:
"I left my spouse for my soul mate."

GOD SAYS:
"What I have joined together, no person should separate."

A man will leave his father and mother and be united to his wife, and the two will become one flesh. So they are no longer two, but one.
MARK 10:7–8

A lovely young woman is facing life with a dull, unloving husband until a handsome stranger rides into town and sweeps her up into an affair. We hope that she will escape her loveless marriage and ride off with her "soul mate."

We've all seen this movie—it is a popular Hollywood plot. And in spite of ourselves, we often end up rooting for infidelity in the name of "true love." Perhaps this story appeals to us because we all long to find our soul mate—someone who knows us so deeply that he or she can fulfill our deepest longings. Desiring this isn't wrong—God created us to want a deep connection with other people. But the world's message is that any means are justified when it comes to finding that soul mate.

The real world doesn't work the way a Hollywood script does, though. When real people break their marriage vows, believing that they have found their soul mate in someone else, the result is only heartache. You see, on your wedding day, a spiritual union is formed. God no longer sees you and your spouse as two separate people, but as one. So in God's eyes, you are soul mates.

Once the wedding is over and real life begins, our feelings of love may begin to fade. We might be tempted to think that things would be better with someone else. The truth is, though, that feelings will always come and go. True love isn't a feeling, but a commitment to act lovingly in spite of our feelings. This isn't easy, but God has joined you together, and He wants to protect your marriage. When you turn to Him for help, He will strengthen your bond. Becoming soul mates takes effort, but it is a goal that is well worth working for and one that God will be faithful to help you achieve.

How good and pleasant it is when [we] live together in unity!
PSALM 133:1

THE WORLD SAYS:
"We have a marriage of convenience."

GOD SAYS:
"The intent of marriage is for two people to become one."

*May the God who gives endurance and encouragement
give you a spirit of unity.*
ROMANS 15:5

When you hear the phrase "a marriage of convenience," perhaps you think of Jane Austen novels in which loveless matches are made for reasons of financial stability or social status. These kinds of arranged unions rarely happen today, at least in the Western world. Many people do, however, find their marriage relationship deteriorating into little more than a convenient way to share expenses and living space.

You never meant for things to get this way. You promised on your wedding day to always love each other deeply and passionately. You wanted to be one of those couples who were still holding hands in public after fifty years together. But the years passed, you had a couple kids, and things got busy. You don't really have time to connect with each other anymore. Frankly, it is simply easier to concentrate on "me," because you just don't have the energy to put into "us."

After a few years, every marriage has its moments of boredom. It's easy to get into a rut. But God created each of us with a great desire for love and intimacy, and He created marriage as a wonderful way to fulfill that desire. He wants your relationship to be full of life and joy so that your marriage will give you a small glimpse into the union He longs to have with you.

A vital, growing marriage doesn't just happen, though. You have to be willing to work together to cultivate your love. Make it a priority to go on a date with your spouse as often as you can. Keep the romance alive with little notes of appreciation or small gifts "just because." And don't forget to pray together and for each other. When you invest in the life of your marriage, you can have a relationship that is captivating rather than just convenient.

How beautiful you are and how pleasing,
O love, with your delights!
Song of Songs 7:6

THE WORLD SAYS:
"I'm looking for someone to take care of me."

GOD SAYS:
"My design is for the two of you to serve each other."

Serve one another in love.
GALATIANS 5:13

Breakfast in bed on your birthday. A gentle back rub after a long day. A warm, home-cooked meal on a cold winter evening. Just reading these phrases makes you smile, doesn't it? The comfort of a loved one is one of the best things in life. Knowing that you have someone who will take care of you when the going gets tough is a wonderful feeling.

God created us to need other people and to find the most fulfillment when we open ourselves up to be loved. But He also created us to give love and care in return. Many people enter into relationships with high expectations of what the other person can do for them. Perhaps you think that because your partner has a good job that he or she will provide for you financially. Or maybe you are longing for a sense of belonging so you see your date as the answer to your loneliness. These are needs that we all have, and it isn't wrong to desire their fulfillment. But if you expect another person to be the answer to the emptiness you sometimes feel, you're going to be disappointed.

No person, no matter how kind, loving, and compassionate they are, can satisfy the deepest longings of your heart. Only God can care for you in a way that will bring you fulfillment and true joy. When you turn to Him, asking for His peace, love, and protection, He will be absolutely faithful to answer you.

Once your heart finds satisfaction in the Lord, you are free to seek out relationships based on mutual love, care, and service. You'll be ready to receive and also equipped to give in return. And this is God's perfect plan for relationships—serving one another out of the abundant life that only He can give.

Your heavenly Father already knows all your needs, and he will give you all you need from day to day if you live for him and make the Kingdom of God your primary concern.

MATTHEW 6:32–33 NLT

THE WORLD SAYS:
"If you want him to love you, give your body to him."

GOD SAYS:
"If you want him to respect you, save yourself for marriage."

Do you not know that your body is a temple of the Holy Spirit, who is in you, whom you have received from God?

1 CORINTHIANS 6:19

The gift is rare and exquisite—the only one of its kind in the whole world. It is priceless. And you own this gift and are in charge of protecting it and choosing the one worthy of receiving it.

Would you give a gift like this to someone in hopes of winning his love, not knowing if he would appreciate it and value it as highly as it deserves? Once this gift is given there is no getting it back, so it must be reserved for the one person who will give it the honor and respect it deserves.

But all around you people are telling you that you don't have to protect your gift. *Don't worry about saving it,* they say. *If you really love someone, then why not go ahead and give it away? You'll prove that you love him if you let him have the gift with no strings attached.*

What is this gift? It is the gift of you—your mind, body, and soul. God created only one you—and because you are so special, you should be extra careful about giving the gift of yourself through sexual intimacy.

Instead of proving your love, when you give yourself to someone sexually outside of a marriage relationship, you are sending the message that you don't expect honor or respect. And when you devalue yourself like this, the person you are giving yourself to won't value you either.

But when you insist on a marriage commitment before giving the gift of yourself, you are demanding the respect and honor you truly deserve. The person who truly loves you will value your gift enough to wait for it. So remember that you are precious and worthy of honor because you are a unique child of God. You are a priceless gift to be given with care!

You are precious and honored in my sight.

Isaiah 43:4

THE WORLD SAYS:
"An affair can give your marriage new life."

GOD SAYS:
"Nothing good can be derived from unfaithfulness and deceit."

Let love and faithfulness never leave you;
bind them around your neck,
write them on the tablet of your heart.
PROVERBS 3:3

The first step in building a new home is to lay a firm foundation. A foundation of the best materials will ensure the stability and long life of the house. When you are building a marriage, a firm foundation of trust, grounded on the stable rock of God's love, will ensure that your relationship will last.

After a few years of wind and rain, every house begins to look a little tired. Perhaps the roof droops a little. Maybe the windows are leaky. These are signs that your house needs some repair to make it solid again. So what do you do? Take a sledgehammer and begin pounding on the foundation? Of course not! And yet, this is exactly what some people do when their marriages get tired and are in need of repair. Instead of putting in the work needed to renew the stability of their union, they take a sledgehammer to their foundation by having an affair.

Perhaps these couples, facing the boredom of a tired marriage, think that an affair will spark jealousy in their spouse and therefore bring their relationship new life. In truth, though, all an affair will do is destroy the foundation of trust that your marriage needs to survive. Without trust, your relationship will crumble and will eventually be destroyed.

If your relationship is showing signs of wear, don't get out the sledgehammer. Do some soul-searching and take time to listen to each other. What repairs need to be made to make your relationship fresh and vital again? Is your communication less than it should be? Make talking to each other daily a priority. Is the romance fading? Go on a weekly date and get to know each other again. When you make the necessary repairs and shore up your foundation of trust, God will bless you with a marriage that will always feel like home.

By wisdom a house is built, and through understanding it is established; through knowledge its rooms are filled with rare and beautiful treasures.

PROVERBS 24:3–4

THE WORLD SAYS:
"Look for a spouse who completes you."

GOD SAYS:
"Only the One who created you can complete you."

[God] who began a good work in you will carry it on to completion until the day of Christ Jesus.

PHILIPPIANS 1:6

Have you ever put together one of those thousand-piece puzzles? It's a challenging endeavor! You begin by putting together the edges and then working on the middle. You glance at the box every once in a while to remind yourself of what the picture is supposed to look like. Sometimes you have a hole in the puzzle and a piece that looks like it should fit. But no matter how hard you try, that piece just isn't the right one. Only one piece will fit that hole, and the puzzle won't be finished until you find it.

Maybe you're working on an even more complicated puzzle right now—the puzzle of your own life. You've been putting together the edges—growing, maturing, getting an education, and working on your career. Now you're beginning to work on the heart of your life. You have a vision of what it is supposed to look like, and you're searching diligently for the pieces that will make that vision complete.

Many people think that the missing piece in the puzzle of their lives is that one perfect man or woman. If only you could find "the one," you would be complete. Then you find that person who seems to be the perfect fit—the picture of your life is finally whole! And yet, no matter how hard you try, even this wonderful person doesn't fill the empty spot inside you. Something is still missing.

The hole in your heart is shaped for only one—and that One is God. He created you with a deep longing to be complete and whole—a longing that only He can fill. He wants that desire to drive you to seek Him and find Him. When you do, He will be found, and that final piece of your life's puzzle will be complete!

[Jesus said,] "I am the vine; you are the branches. Those who remain in me, and I in them, will produce much fruit."

JOHN 15:5 NLT

THE WORLD SAYS:
*"He/she is the love
of my life."*

GOD SAYS:
*"I am the everlasting love in
both of your lives."*

"I have loved you with an everlasting love."
JEREMIAH 31:3

Turn on the radio any time of the day or night, and you are sure to hear a love song. Bookstores are full of books with titles that promise success in romance. Everywhere you turn, the world is telling you that finding the love of your life will make you happy and fulfilled. And it is true that falling in love is wonderful. Surely, finding that one true love will satisfy all your longings, and you'll live happily ever after!

The unfortunate fact is, though, that none of us is perfect, and sooner or later, we fail each other. In spite of our best efforts, we cause those we love the most disappointment and hurt. Putting your heart completely in the care of another person will never give you the kind of love that you so deeply desire. That's why God asks that you give Him your whole heart—only He can fill it with everlasting love that does not disappoint.

God created you for one special purpose above all else—to be the love of His life. Among all the wonders of creation, from the snowcapped mountains to the majestic eagle, you are God's masterpiece. The entire Bible is God's love letter to you—written so that you could know and love Him. And in the ultimate show of love, God, in the form of Jesus, came to earth to die for you, so that you might be able to live forever with Him.

Have you been trying desperately to find "the one"—that man or woman who will be the love of your life? Or have you found someone, only to be disappointed when he or she didn't fill the emptiness in your heart? Then turn to the Lover of your soul—God. He is the everlasting love of your life.

May [God] grant your heart's desire.
PSALM 20:4 NLT

THE WORLD SAYS:
"Marriage kills sex."

GOD SAYS:
"Marriage creates true intimacy."

"Arise, my darling,
my beautiful one, and come with me.
See! The winter is past;
the rains are over and gone.
Flowers appear on the earth;
the season of singing has come."
SONG OF SONGS 2:10–12

Jack and Rose in *Titanic*. Viola and Will in *Shakespeare in Love*. Neo and Trinity in *The Matrix*. These movies all portray exciting and wildly passionate relationships between unmarried couples. Then you turn on the TV, and you see what happens after these passionate couples tie the knot—or at least what Hollywood says happens. Every night of the week, you'll find a sitcom with a bumbling and usually overweight husband and an overworked and sharp-tongued wife. Rarely are they portrayed as having anything but a mediocre relationship, at best. The message seems to be that once you're married, sex is boring or nonexistent.

God Himself dispels this myth, though, by giving us a glimpse into a truly passionate, even steamy, marriage relationship in the Bible. Song of Songs, sometimes called Song of Solomon, is the story of Solomon and his beautiful new wife. It begins with the young bride asking her husband to take her away with him to his chamber. Throughout this passionate book, the newlyweds praise each other's looks: her beautiful eyes, hair, and yes, even her breasts; his strong arms, manly physique, and even his prowess in the bedroom! Did you know that was in the Bible?

The fact that God included this explicit book in His Word is proof that He wants us to have great sex within the intimacy of marriage. God created sexual pleasure—it is the physical manifestation of the spiritual union that you make on your wedding day, when the two of you become one. It allows you to show each other love in a way that is unique to your relationship alone. When you reserve sex for your marriage alone, you'll find that it is more fulfilling than you ever imagined it could be. Far from killing the passion, marriage gives sex a depth and a fire that has no equal.

I belong to my lover, and his desire is for me.
Song of Songs 7:10

THE WORLD SAYS:
"A woman has the right to choose."

GOD SAYS:
"Choose life."

*My frame was not hidden from you
when I was made in the secret place.
When I was woven together in the depths of the earth,
your eyes saw my unformed body.*

PSALM 139:15–16

A battle has been waging for many years in the United States over the issue of abortion. People have strong feelings and opinions on both sides of the issue. Have you ever wondered what God thinks about the issue of abortion? The Bible doesn't speak specifically about this procedure, but it does give us God's perspective on life and choice. God has given you the ability to choose. No matter what a government decrees, as a human being, made in the image of God, you have been given choice—free will. God will not force you to follow Him or to do what He wants you to do. So, in truth, you do have the right to choose.

On the other side of the issue is God's view of life. God is the Creator, and His creation is precious to Him. He says that He knows you even as you are growing inside your mother's womb. He calls you His masterpiece. Surely He feels great sadness when the life of one of His tiny new creations is cut short by abortion. His heart also aches for the mother who will now have to face the painful consequences of her choice.

The Bible reveals to us what God thinks about the issue of abortion through His words about both life and choice. Each unborn child is His creation. And every mother is also His child. His heart longs for her to choose life. When she does, she will be protected from the terrible pain that comes with abortion and will experience the overwhelming joy of bringing a new person into the world.

So when it comes to abortion, God says, "Yes, you do have the right to choose." But He also says, "Choose life—for the sake of your child, and for your own sake as well, My precious daughter."

Choose life, so that you and your children may live.
DEUTERONOMY 30:19

THE WORLD SAYS:
"It's okay to have cyber sex."

GOD SAYS:
"Whatsoever things are good, holy, just. . .think on these things."

Whatever is true, whatever is noble, whatever is right, whatever is pure, whatever is lovely, whatever is admirable—if anything is excellent or praiseworthy—think about such things.

PHILIPPIANS 4:8

Once there was a little boy who liked to play in the woods. The boy's father warned him repeatedly to steer clear of any snakes he came across because they might be poisonous. The little boy assured his father that he would heed the warning.

But secretly, the little boy was intrigued with the reptiles. When he was playing in the woods alone, he would often watch them slither along the leafy ground. Soon he was reaching out his finger and touching the snakes. Then, the boy decided he would try, just once, to catch one of them.

But, of course, you know how the story ends. The boy grabs the serpent and gets bitten. As his hand throbs with pain, he remembers his father's warning and wishes that he had listened. The excitement of playing with the snake was not worth the pain of the bite.

The "forest" of the Internet is a great place to play, but it, too, is full of poisonous snakes in the form of pornography. These sites may seem harmless—you're just looking. No one is getting hurt. But one evening of looking leads to another and another. Before you know it, you're feeling the pain of the bite—your relationship is crumbling, your boss has written you up, and you begin to feel that your life is out of control.

Your heavenly Father has warned you through His Word to stay away from "snakes" like cyber sex. He's not trying to spoil your fun—He wants to protect you from pain. Instead, He calls you to fill your mind with things that are pure, beautiful, and holy—things that will bring you true joy. Pornography is dangerous, and like a poisonous snake, it can destroy you before you realize what happened. Heed your Father's warning and ask for His protection. He is faithful to help you.

Above all else, guard your heart, for it is the wellspring of life.
PROVERBS 4:23

LOVE

I love you,
Not only for what you are,
But for what I am when I am with you.

I love you,
Not only for what you have made of yourself,
But for what you are making of me.

I love you
For the part of me that you bring out;
I love you
For putting your hand into my heaped-up heart
And passing over all the foolish, weak things
That you can't help dimly seeing there,
And for drawing out into the light
All the beautiful belongings that no one else had looked
Quite far enough to find.

I love you
Because you are helping me to make
Of the lumber of my life
Not a tavern
But a temple;
Out of the works of my every day
Not a reproach
But a song.

Author Unknown

Also Available from Barbour Publishing

Searching for the right road in a world full of false
twists and turns? This powerful book helps you
discover God's answers to the questions in your heart.

Truth.
Seeing Black and White in a Gray World
1-59789-104-5

Available Wherever Books Are Sold.